HISTORIC CHURCHES OF AMERICA

The Old South Church, Boston, Massachusetts

HISTORIC CHURCHES OF AMERICA

BY
NELLIE URNER WALLINGTON

INTRODUCTION BY
EDWARD EVERETT HALE

NEW YORK
DUFFIELD & COMPANY
1907

Copyright, 1907, by

DUFFIELD & COMPANY

Published September, 1907

CONTENTS

CONTENTS

LIST OF ILLUSTRATIONS

INTRODUCTION

ONE does not go back in any study of the local history of any part of the United States without finding himself engaged in ecclesiastical study, or in what is generally called the history of religion. Indeed, this is of course when we consider how closely the discovery of America followed the invention of printing. For the history of America becomes contemporary with the history of that revolution in ecclesiastical affairs which we call the Reformation, which was in itself the immediate result of the invention of printing. Thus the life of Christopher Columbus is the life of a devout religious man. When you come to his motive, even in details where you would hardly expect it, you find tokens of his loyalty to the religious thought and instruction of his time.

Mrs. Wallington's book, which I introduce cordially to the reader, will trace in some detail the first steps which were taken in different parts of the nation by persons of distinct religious motive who had exiled themselves from Europe and who meant to maintain their allegiance to the living God. In those emigrations, which were distinctly made because the emigrants wanted a closer walk with God, the great results have been worthy of their origin. Nobody who knows what he is talking about pretends to say that in the birth of every European colony here a religious motive was the only motive. But this is certain, that in every colony which as it grew made any important contribution to the life of the America of to-day, the religious training of the colonists is to be the subject of the first study.

The Island of Puerto Rico, the latest addition to our territory, has our oldest monuments of European or Christian civilisation. The Spanish settlement at St. Augustine, Florida, was made as early as 1565. The settlement in Santa Fé in New Mexico was begun perhaps even earlier than that of St. Augustine. But in 1680 the Indians, whom they had reduced to slavery, revolted, drove out the Spaniards, and burned their churches and archives. The present city of Santa Fé dates back to the year 1692. Of some of the earliest of these settlements of the sixteenth century, the existence was so short that we have not even the ruins of their places of worship. Sir Walter Raleigh sent out his North Carolina Colony in 1584. Doubtless those settlers maintained religious worship on Roanoke Island. But there are hardly any vestiges of their short-lived occupation. Before that time, the Spaniards had attempted to colonise the western shore of Chesapeake Bay. But by a singular turn of the wheel of fortune, on which perhaps the history of the world changed, the winter proved to be one of exceptional severity. Those men who were used to the West Indies and to Spain could not bear its severity and so soon as the ice left their rivers the Spaniards prepared to remove to a gentler climate.

While England had a paper claim, or afterwards pretended that she had because of Cabot's discovery of the eastern coast of the United States in 1496, the English sovereigns made no attempt to take possession of the continent on the Atlantic side before the enterprise of Raleigh. On the Pacific side Drake had planted a cross and taken possession of northern California in the name of Queen Elizabeth as early as 1579. But meanwhile, in the interior, the Mexican Viceroys had pushed up as far as Santa Fé.

In the early years of the seventeenth century the Frenchmen had established fishing settlements which outlived the winters, in the regions which surround what we now call by the name which they gave them, Mount Desert and Frenchmen's Bay. But Mrs. Wallington can give us no account of the ruins of their churches, for we do not even know where they were. In 1602 the Earl of Southampton sent the *Concord* along the New England shore, and for a few weeks her captain, Gosnold, thought he had es-

tablished a settlement on Cuttyhunk Island, at
the opening of Buzzard's Bay, in Massachusetts.
But it was but a short-lived colony. Doubtless
there were Sunday services there, but there was
no church, and with early autumn the colonists,
who had quarrelled among themselves. returned
to England.

In the year 1607, under a charter of King
James the First, what is known as the Popham
Colony was established near the mouth of the
Kennebec River. Worship was maintained there
for the few months of its existence. But no man
knows where was the altar which was established
for so short a time.

With the arrival of Captains Newport and
Smith in the James River and the establishment
of Jamestown, which we are celebrating in this
year 1907, begins the history of Christian worship conducted regularly by Englishmen for
three centuries.

With the varied history of the Spanish foun-
dations, of the arrival of French Huguenots in
Carolina and in Florida, then the settlements at
Roanoke Island and Jamestown, afterwards the
establishments of the Dutch in Manhattan, with
the subsequent arrival of the Puritans in New
England, of the Swedes in the Delaware, of
Penn on the west bank of that river, with the
settlements of French pioneers in Detroit and
Vincennes, and with their later establishments in

Louisiana, with Oglethorpe's colony in Georgia, the history of organised Christianity in the United States goes forward until the close of the eighteenth century. Since that time, emigrants have arrived here from almost every climate, of all faiths and of none. The Russian Doukhobor, the Congo negro, the coolie from China, the Nestorian from Mesopotamia, with a hundred others, bring their varied contributions to the religion of America.

Antoine Las Casas, a soldier in the marine service of Spain, accompanied Columbus in the great voyage which has given such distinction to the year 1492. His son Bartholomew, who won the great distinction of being the first Christian missionary who devoted himself to the service of the Master in America, was completing his studies at the University of Salamanca. In 1498, at the age of twenty-four, he went to the West Indies with his father under Columbus. He returned to Cadiz in 1500. In 1502 he sailed for the second time with Columbus for San Domingo. In 1510 he was ordained priest by the first bishop of Hispaniola, and he said his virgin mass in the capital city.

The first Dominican monks under their bishop, Cordova, reached that island in the same year. "We shall find," says Dr. Ellis, "that the Dominicans were from the first and always firm friends, approvers, and helpers of Las Casas in the hard conflict for asserting the rights of humanity for the outraged natives." And it is, as Dr. Ellis says, " One of the strange phenomena in history that the founders and prime agents of the Inquisition in Europe should be the champions of the heathen in the new world."

In 1561 the King of Spain determined that no further attempt should be made to colonise the continent north of Cuba, either in the Gulf or at St. Helena. But the very next year a colony of French Huguenots founded Charles Fort under Ribault, and for four years that colony maintained itself. In 1565, however, the Spanish commander Menendez resented this interference, attacked the French fort, and stormed it. In 1565 the Frenchman de Gourgues resented and revenged this success by an invasion in which he destroyed the little post and hanged his prisoners, " not as to Spaniards," he said, " but as to traitors, robbers and murderers." But in the next year Menendez renewed the colony which maintained itself until the village was destroyed by Drake. It was rebuilt, however, and dates from 1572, as the oldest of American cities on the Atlantic seaboard.

The careful reader of the history of the United States will learn from Mr. Fiske's admirable account of the early history of Virginia how the establishment of English settlers in the regions of Virginia was due to the religious as well as to the political determination of Raleigh and his English successors. The hatred of Spain to which their generation of Englishmen was bred became a matter of religion. The young noblemen and gentlemen of England who went cordially into the affairs of American colonisation worked under impulses not unlike those which stimulated the young students of Williams College, when they highly determined to consecrate their lives to the conversion of the heathen.

One of the last words addressed by John Robinson, the minister of the Plymouth Colony, expressed his interest in the work of Christian Missions. "I wish you had converted some of them before you had slain any." With the arrival of John Eliot, a young Puritan preacher from England, a definite and well-organised missionary work for such conversion began. A society was formed of religious men in England, to raise money and to send out men to America. It still exists in London. It is not fair to say that it was unsuccessful. And between that time and this, the history of all the American States gives us details of the work of consecrated men and women who have addressed themselves specifically to this Christian duty. Eliot himself, was as is now well known, an accurate student of language. He and his pupils translated the whole English Bible into the language of the Massachusetts Indians, and the English society

paid the expenses of printing and publishing
it.*

The language of the Massachusetts chosen
for this translation belongs to the language of
the Algonquin Indians, the branch of their race
most widely dispersed in North America. The
Algonquin language was spoken by all the Indians of New England, by those in Long Island
and on the seaboard so far south as North Carolina. An Indian from Massachusetts Bay would
have understood Powhatan or Pocahontas, or the
Delaware Indians, with whom William Penn
dealt, as well as a Spaniard understands an Ital-
ian to-day. And at this hour an educated gen-
tleman of the Ojibwa tribe, close by Duluth, can
entertain himself and his children by spelling out
the words of the Sermon on the Mount, not un-
familiar to them, as they find them in Eliot's
Bible.

As the European nations began to know more
and more of the Atlantic border of America the
missionary spirit showed itself in the effort of
hundreds of their enthusiasts to write on the
white paper which they found in a new land.

At the moment when persecution in Austria
distressed the Moravian brethren of Count Zinzendorf, General Oglethorpe and the other founders of Georgia were able to offer them " free-

* A full and accurate dictionary of this important book by the
late J. Hammond Trumbull has recently been published.

dom to worship God " in the beautiful regions
which they had taken in hand. The establishment of Bethlehem, in the northern part of
Pennsylvania, by a Moravian Colony is another
of the enterprises, romantic from end to end,
which were undertaken by the Moravian fra-
ternity. Before the century was over many religious establishments, some now forgotten, some
prosperous under the free worship of American
life, established themselves in one and another
region under the auspices of Christian adventurers.

It would be a very little thing to invite the
reader to recall a few facts of external history in
the organisation of the different churches which
have formed themselves in the different origins
of America. Mrs. Wallington has not satisfied
herself with any such showman's exhibits of the
slides in the box of his camera. The history of
these churches takes us back—I may say of
course—to the great central duties to which their
leaders have addressed themselves in building up
the country. It is the history of the power of
the moral forces. Such is the phrase of people
who like to play with scholastic words. It is the
history which shows that the Power which makes
for righteousness is the supreme Power, which
makes indeed a new revelation of itself with the
passage of every century. Nowhere is that les-
son more easily read than it can be read in the

history of this nation, where, as I said, the good God had white paper to write upon.

And it will be observed that the advance of the country from century to century has not been dependent, no, not in one single step, on the external forms or methods of these churches. Forms and methods have their place, so many grains of sand torn up from one ocean-beaten floor to be flung upon another. But the good God does not reveal Himself in the form; His kingdom comes as He speaks in the still, small voice which was not in tempest, in thunders, in lightnings, or in earthquakes.

Catholic, Huguenot, Lutheran, Calvinist, Englishman, Scotchman, Irishman, German, or Dutch,—whatever these settlers called themselves, whatever uniform they chose to wear, there were among them men who walked with God,—or tried to. They loved justice, they loved mercy, and they walked humbly with Him. If they were tempted by merely rhetorical expression to make clear to men what is this Walk with God, they certainly failed. If they supposed that the Infinite Life could be revealed by nominative cases and by verbs in any of the forms of grammar, they failed. It proved that language is a matter of things. But every man who accepted the inspiration of the Holy Spirit succeeded. It is the fine phrase of William Bradford, which says of the men who landed on

Plymouth Rock, that they " agreed to walk together." They did not prescribe any form of
worship, they did not attempt any hard and fast
definition in words of the Faith and Hope and
Love which are eternal. For the Infinite, because it is infinite, cannot be defined. But they
walked together and they walked with God. So
He lent them His own omnipotence for their
success.

As a single illustration of such success we need
not be afraid to cite the details of their dealings
with the native tribes whom they found here.
There has been a great deal of exaggerated mis-
statement as to the relations of the white men
and the red men with each other. And it is easy
to sneer at the European emigrant as driving
very hard bargains when he bought principalities,
perhaps, for a few red coats or a few axes, with
a few beads and other trinkets. From such
sneers there springs up a school of invective
which would make us believe that the American
pioneers were more savage than the red man
whom they crushed, and that the children of nature were cruelly oppressed by men who sought
simply their own profit or credit. Such sneers
have undoubtedly for their confirmation legends
which are true of the exasperating outrages com-
mitted by frontier traders or other adventurers
who were utterly careless of human life.

But it is not true in any single instance of the

history of the American States that the governors or leaders of those States have had any policy of extermination or any wish of oppression. Such leaders had come here intending to stay. Such leaders have stayed, and because they have stayed, for better for worse, the United States of America exists to-day. But they had no reason to propose the destruction of the native races, nor has any company of them ever attempted the policy of destruction. If such an alliance as King Philip formed in New England proposed and expected to drive the newly-landed colonists into the sea and to destroy their towns, those colonists, one might say of course, had to stand on their defence with no pretence of gentleness in their vigour. If Lancaster were destroyed by the Indians in Massachusetts we are not to wonder if some Indian fortress were stormed and the village it protected was burned. But this happened, not because the Massachusetts colonists meant to destroy the Indians. There was room enough for white men and for red men, and it is not fair to ascribe events which sprang from the fortunes of war to a preconceived purpose of extermination.

No! The history of the three centuries is the history on the part of the leaders of the whites of attempts for the improvement and the civilisation of the tribes whom they found here. Grant that they seem foolish sometimes as we look back upon them, but the men who planned them did not think they were foolish. It is foolish for us now to pay rations or pensions which encourage idleness and laziness among Indian tribes, but the men who made the treaties which bind us to such lavish expenditure did not think that they were foolish, and did not make them with the intent of debasing the men with whom they were dealing.

And to sum up in a few words what the policy has resulted in which the Governors of America have pursued with frequent changes, but with good purposes, it ought to be enough to say, that according to the best authorities, more men and women of the native tribes are living within our territory now than ever lived here before. Their powers for war and mutual slaughter are less, their powers and skill in the works of civilisation are greater. And though one enterprise and another for what has been thought to be their elevation and improvement have wretchedly failed, yet, on the whole, the boy or girl born in an Indian tribe in our day has a better chance for the best which life has to offer than such a boy or girl ever had before.

And to speak in a few words only, I shall best introduce Mrs. Wallington's curious and interesting book to the Christian reader by reminding him that although many outside forms of religion are represented here the great success which makes the civilised America of to-day has sprung from the practical union of the religious men and women of every communion.

For it is to be noticed that with every aggressive enterprise against any of the works of the devil or against the ignorance of a world which has not liked "to retain God in its knowledge," you find this central wish,—to walk together with other children of God. You do not find prominent the expression of intellectual opinion or a reference to the history of the past. Whatever the enterprise of reform which is undertaken, whether it be in education, in temperance, in bringing God to men and men to God more closely, the men interested have wished " to go about doing good." If they have had any creed it was simply that they would proclaim on the right hand and on the left hand that the kingdom of God is at hand. They have been enthusiastic in their Master's service. But they remembered that the description of Him given by His apostles was that He went about doing good. They remembered that His promises were given not to the men who cried Lord, Lord, but for those who remembered to do the things of which He spoke.

Mrs. Wallington's book expresses fitly what we must hope that the twentieth century will show to America,—namely, that the religion of the twentieth century is to be a religion of action rather than of historical expression. It is a religion of man working with God and God working with man. It will have less and less to say about " I believe in this," or " I believe in that." It will have more and more of that spirit in which men will walk together, and that they will walk humbly with their God.

EDWARD E. HALE.

HISTORIC CHURCHES
OF AMERICA

THE OLD SOUTH CHURCH

MOST famous of all historic churches in
our country is, perhaps, the Old
South Meeting House in Boston,
within whose walls in colonial and Revolutionary times were spoken some of the boldest words
of patriotism, and from whose rostrum went up
the strongest of the appeals that fanned into
flame the fire that drove the British from
America.

From the very founding of the Massachusetts
Colony there had existed a close union between
church and state; none could be freemen except
church members and none but freemen were
entitled to the ballot. Since the number of non-
church members increased annually, such a condition of affairs created more and more dissat-
isfaction, and as early as 1646, twenty-six years
after the founding of the Colony, a petition
was sent to the General Court asking a removal
of this religious disability. It is one of the
many glories of the Old South Church that it
originated this initial struggle to separate
church and state. The General Court declined to grant the petition of the non-church

members, and finally an official council, which
met in Boston in June, 1657, declared that all
baptised persons were entitled to the same privileges at the ballot-box as church members.   In
1662 a General Synod was convened to discuss
the matter, at which the members failed to agree,
but recommended the continuance of the existing conditions.   The First Church of Boston,
an earlier organisation, accepted this recom-
mendation, but twenty-nine of its members,
including the most respectable among the residents of the city, seceded and formed a separate church organisation.   In accordance with
the prevailing custom, it was necessary to gain
the consent of the church to such secession,
which, however, the church denied.   Nothing
daunted, the secessionists asked permission of
the Governor of the State to erect a place of
worship, and, failing to obtain his permission,
they next petitioned the selectmen of Boston,
who granted their request.   They accordingly
erected a meeting house of cedar, two stories
in height, with a steeple, and modest interior,
with the conventional high-backed square pews
and lofty pulpit of olden church times.   Until
October 16, 1674, the wives, mothers and daughters of the twenty-nine male members still worshipped with the First Church, being forbidden
by that organisation to sever their connection
with it.   It was not until the General Council

Ruins at Jamestown, Virginia

estant service in America was held. The offici-
ating clergyman was the Reverend Robert Hunt,
and the service was that of the Established
Church of England. Until homes were erected
for the colonists and better shelter provided,
this rude temple with its canvas roof and seats
of unsawn timber served as a place to worship
God, and here divine service was held twice on
each Sabbath day.

A few days after the debarkation of the colonists Captain John Smith set out on a voyage
of discovery, and until his return no attempt
seems to have been made to provide a more suitable church building. After his return from the
exploration of the James River, with that strenu-
ousness that marked all his procedures, Captain
Smith undertook the erection of a structure in
which the colonists might worship God with
greater comfort in stormy weather. He described this church as a "homely thing, like a
barn set on crutches and covered with rafts,
sedge and earth, as were also the walls." But
the dwelling houses were similarly constructed,
and with even greater rudeness. In this new
"house of God" sermon and prayer were heard
daily, both morning and evening, two services
on each Sabbath, and communion every three
months, until the death of the Reverend Robert
Hunt.

One special injunction had been laid by the

London company upon Captain Smith, to make
a rigid exploration of every stream he found
that emptied into the Atlantic Ocean, with the
hope that a short route would be discovered to
the Pacific.   Soon after the erection of the
" church upon stilts " he undertook another voyage of discovery, and during this absence the
little church was destroyed by fire.   Upon his
return Captain Smith was elected President of
the little colony, and employing the authority
his new position gave him he commanded that
the work of building a domicile for himself,
which the colonists had planned and begun during his absence, he discontinued until a new
church had been erected.   Under his personal
supervision this new church was nearing completion when the wounds that he had received in a
conflict with the Indians compelled him to sail
to England for surgical treatment.

With the departure of Captain Smith the
more lawless among the colonists, whom his in-
trepid spirit had so far kept in check, broke loose
in unbridled rioting.   The Indians, too, no
longer coerced by his presence, and daily in-
flamed by the treatment accorded them, became
hostile in their attitude.   Plantations were laid
waste, and provisions became so exhausted that
famine stared the colonists in the face.   Wholly
disheartened, they embarked for England, but
when they neared the mouth of the James River

they met Lord Delaware, bringing provisions and reinforcements from England. Returning to the former settlement, under the wise rule of Lord Delaware they soon conquered the Indians and held them in check, while the colony prospered under strict government. The little church that Captain Smith had begun was finished, and with wise forethought Lord Delaware employed in its fitting and furnishings the choicest woods that the Virginia forests afforded. The communion table and altar were constructed of black walnut, while the shutters, the pews and the pulpit were made of cedar; the baptismal font was "hewn hollow like a canoe." Services were again instituted, being conducted by the Reverend Mr. Buckle, who had been sent from England to succeed Mr. Hunt. Daily service was begun, and daily the little altar was decorated with the native wild flowers of Virginia. The Governor, Lord Delaware, never failed in his attendance, and invariably appeared in the full dignity of velvet and lace, with a bodyguard clad in rich attire and scarlet cloaks.

A full-toned bell, brought from England, was hung in the belfry, and not only served to call the colonists to worship, but gave notice to the little industrial army when to begin and when to leave off work for the day.

In that little church, which owed its existence to Captain John Smith, the Indian maiden, Pocahontas, was baptised in the Christian faith in April, 1614, and following the ceremony her marriage took place with the colonist, John Rolfe, whose wife had succumbed to the hardships of the rude life in the colony. The marriage was celebrated in the presence of an amicable company of Indians and Englishmen. One could wish that there were more details concerning this first marriage contracted between an Englishman and a native-born princess of America. How much weight this alliance may have had with the Indians it would be difficult to estimate, but at least the Virginia settlers gained eight years of freedom from Indian attacks.

In 1639 a solid brick church succeeded the little wooden structure, the dimensions of the new edifice being fifty-six by twenty-eight feet. In front of the new church building and joined to it, forming the front entrance, was built a square tower, reaching from the ground to the full height of the edifice. By the time this later building was completed the Virginia colonists had obtained greater security from Indian molestation. In the little adjoining churchyard were successively buried the Governors of Virginia who died in office, as well as the rectors who in turn served the little parish.

In 1676 Nathaniel Bacon instigated the most widespread rebellion with which Virginia had yet had to cope. Bacon was a man bred to the law, and by reason of his talents as well as by his great ambition had easily gained a position in the Virginia Council, not to mention attaining the rank of Colonel in the Virginia militia. Rebelling against the authority of Governor Berkeley, he advanced toward Jamestown, and civil war—the first in America—resulted. In retaliation for the dishonour he conceived was planned against him by the act of Governor Berkeley in placing a price upon his head, Bacon applied the torch to Jamestown, reducing it to ashes. Nothing remained standing but the ruins of the little church tower and a few solitary, blackened chimneys.

No later attempt was made to erect a church building upon this site, and even to-day the ruins of the tower are picturesque in their desolation. The wash of the tide has gradually removed the sand that joined " Sandy Beach," the site of the edifice, with the mainland, and the spot where Jamestown once stood is an island which is gradually being worn away. Unless sufficient precautionary measures are taken, this first and most ancient landmark of the Protestant Church in America will disappear.

ST. PETER'S

WHITEHOUSE, VIRGINIA

THE character of the early settlers of Virginia revealed itself. in their houses of worship, which differed materially from the severely plain meeting-houses built by the Puritans in New England. The churches erected by the residents of the Old Dominion suggested luxury and comfort, though money was as scarce among them as with the settlers further north. Among the Virginians tobacco served as an equivalent of money, and when the English settlers of New Kent County decided to build a house of worship at Whitehouse, in 1703, they paid for its erection by contributions of the fragrant weed.

The church of St. Peter's was built in the form of a parallelogram. At one end rose a tower, square in shape and capped with a steeple, with a weather vane above, made in representation of the keys of St. Peter. In architectural style the church repeated the old English parish churches, and doubtless recalled to the minds of its earlier communicants the green fields and well-trimmed hedges of "merrie England."

Within the building the pulpit was raised high above the heads of the congregation; above it hung the ever-present sounding-board and upon a bracket beside it stood the inevitable hourglass. The communicants occupied family pews, a practice which differed from that of many churches further north, in which the men sat on one side of the house of worship and the women upon the other. In St. Peter's the individual pews were of liberal dimensions and were provided with the high backs in vogue at that time.

The communicants came to church from many miles around, the family coaches bringing the elders, while the younger members rode on horseback. A gallery was provided for the negro slaves, who waited at the door in winter, each with a foot-stove full of hot embers to keep warm the extremities of his master and mistress. Upon the arrival of the owners the slaves followed them to their respective pews, and only after a careful placing of the foot-stoves did the negroes think of seeking their own seats in the gallery.

After service the good Virginians, always a social people, collected in groups and passed the time in friendly converse, while the negro servants brought the riding horses and the coaches round to the door.

Of such importance was St. Peter's Church, not only spiritually, but socially as well, that it

was selected as the scene of one of the historical
events of Virginia—the marriage in 1759 of
George Washington and Mrs. Martha Custis.
One can picture to one's self the pomp of such
a marriage, what with the wealth of the bride
and the high social standing of each of the con-
tracting parties.

With such loving care and with so deep reverence has St. Peter's Church been preserved
that even the tides of war have left no marks
upon it; it still stands, mellow with past glory
and a quaint suggestion of antiquity, and regularly the communicants of the parish gather for
services in it each Sabbath.

THE OLD NORTH CHURCH

PORTSMOUTH, NEW HAMPSHIRE

CONSIDERING the simple materials at the command of its builders in 1657 one must admit the first church building erected in Portsmouth, New Hampshire, to have been a most substantial structure. It was, at any rate, though crude and simple in construction and comfortless in its interior, enough to answer the requirements of the congregation for fifty years, before they decided to erect a more pretentious house of worship. This they did in 1708, choosing the site upon another corner of the church glebe.

In order to provide protection from Indian attacks, the original little meeting-house had been placed on the hill only a few rods from the south milldam. It boasted a glebe of some fifty acres, but had no regular minister, relying wholly on the services of travelling missionaries. The first ordained minister, the Reverend Mr. Moody, entered upon his labours in 1671, and in addition to regular services on the Sabbath, weekly meetings were held at the houses of the members of the church.

The little church was the scene of all town meetings, and even its ledger was called into requisition to record the number of wolves' heads that were brought in for bounty. These heads were nailed on the meeting-house door as substantial evidence that the claimant was entitled to his reward.

The Governor of the Colony, who was a staunch Episcopalian, brought to bear against the Congregational minister the provisions of the Act of Conformity of King Charles II. Governor Cranfield himself attended service in the Old North Church, as it came to be called, and personally investigated the matter, with the result that the minister was sent to jail in 1683, only to be released thirteen weeks later upon his agreeing to leave the Colony. The blow that thus fell upon the Reverend Mr. Moody was felt most keenly by every member of the little congregation. He went to Boston to serve one of the more enterprising churches there for ten years, but his heart remained with the little flock at Portsmouth, to whom he returned, finally, and whom he served for four years more until his death.

From the time of the building of the new church in 1708 the congregation desired a clock and bell for their meeting-house, though not till 1749 were they able to accomplish their desire. On March 25 the new clock was set up in the

The Old North Church, Portsmouth, New Hampshire

steeple, and its ability to strike the hours proved most gratifying to all the residents of Portsmouth village. A bell, too, had been procured and hung in the belfry.

In 1835 a still more modern house of worship was erected, to which the bell, the clock, and most of the furnishings of the old meeting-house were duly transferred. The church was thoroughly renovated in 1855, the alterations being so extensive as to be practically a rebuilding. The following year the parish purchased a modern clock and sent the old bell to England to be recast, to the great regret of the congregation ever since, as the vessel, with all its cargo, was lost at sea.

The Old North Church has had a happy history, escaping even from the turmoil and depredation that befel other houses of God during the turbulent days of the Revolution. Few churches in America show in their annals a greater spirit of harmony among their members. No schisms have arisen, and there has been a steady growth in the even tenor of its way, undisturbed by rivalries and dissensions.

TRINITY CHURCH

WILMINGTON, DELAWARE

WHEN William Penn came to America he found colonies of Swedes who, for half a century, had tilled the soil of Pennsylvania and Delaware, as well as of the Western shores of New Jersey. These Swedish colonists were assisted in their emigration by William Uselin, who obtained from the King of Sweden permission to found colonies along the shores of the Delaware River. The land was purchased from the Indians and the first Swedish colony planted at the mouth of Christina Creek in 1627. Here they erected a small church to which all the settlers in the Swedish colonies at Lewistown and Tinicum came for service including their governor, John Prinz, who had built for himself a pretentious mansion which he named "Prinz Hall." The pew the governor occupied in the little church was decorated to suit the pomp of the gubernatorial position. The settlers named their cluster of colonies "New Sweden," still maintaining allegiance to the Old World government.

The simple structure erected by the Swedes as a house for divine worship served their needs until 1699, when the building showed unmistakable signs of decay, and amid the tears of many of the communicants service was held in it for the last time.

One year earlier, John Statcop, one of the church wardens in the Colony, had given the church a tract of land for a church site and a glebe. On May 28, 1698, the erection of the new church was begun, and by Trinity Sunday, 1699, it was completed. Upon this same Trinity Sunday the church was dedicated. The fact that the building cost some eight hundred pounds is sufficient evidence that these humble settlers had prospered materially since their settlements upon American soil.

The dimensions of the new church, which was built of granite, were sixty by thirty feet, and the building rose to a height of twenty feet in all. In order to render it durable the stone walls were made six feet thick at the foundation and three feet at the level of the windows. There were five large arched windows, and arched doors to give ample ingress and egress. In the front wall of the church were inserted iron letters bearing the inscription:

1698
SI DEUS PRO NOBIS, QUIS CONTRA NOS.
Sub. Imp. Reg. D. G. Aug.
WILL III
Prop. Will. Penn. Bice – Gub. Will
Magnif, Reg. Suec. Nunc, Glor. Nemor.
CAROL XI
Huc. Ablig.
E. T. B.
W. S.
P. L.

On the eastern gable is a Latin sentence which translated, reads, "The light arising from on high shines in the darkness."

The church was consecrated with all solemnity. Upon the following Christmas matins were held, as well as upon Easter Sunday and the Day of Pentecost. On each occasion the church was garlanded and side lights were introduced to add to the attractiveness of the event. These additional lights were provided by pine torches, which must have contributed to the excitement, especially of those whose duty it was to watch over them. A belfry was projected for the structure, but it was not completed, and the church bell was suspended, temporarily, from a huge walnut tree which grew close by.

The pews were distributed according to services rendered in the erection of the building, and not according to wealth or social rank. They became also inalienable inheritances in the families of the original owners, descending from father to son. They could, if need arose, be sold, and, in case of the removal or dying out of a family, reverted by law to the church.

Among the most highly prized possessions of Trinity Church is a large eucharistic cup, together with a paten and wafer box of silver, which were sent out from Sweden in 1718 as a gift to the parish. These are still regularly used at communion.

In 1735 it was decided by the Swedish colonists that a town should be built upon the church lands. Adjoining the glebe was an immense tract belonging to an Englishman named. Thomas Willing. Master Willing gladly joined hands with the church vestry in this undertaking, and as the first house was erected upon his section of the town site, the name given to the locality was Willingstown. Later, when the village was incorporated, the name was changed to Wilmington, in honor of the English earl.

After the death of the Swedish pastor, the Reverend Mr. Tranberg, in 1748, the parish contained so large a number of English-speaking members among the communicants that it was decided to conduct each alternate service in English.

On April 16, 1750, a meeting of the parish was called to consider the best method of strengthening the walls of the church, which in

spite of their three feet of thickness had begun
to yield under the heavy weight of the roof.
Through some oversight or lack of constructive
knowledge on the part of the builders, this roof
had neither arch nor beams, and there was nothing to bind together the upper portions of the
wall. The south wall was rebuilt and a new roof
was constructed. During these changes additional windows were introduced to obtain more
light in the church.

In 1792, so much had the English-speaking
people increased among the communicants that
it was decided, after due deliberation, to adopt
the ritual of the Protestant Episcopal Church,
and Trinity Church of Wilmington sought and
secured admission into the Diocese of Delaware
of that denomination.

On May 28, 1899, the church of the " Old
Swedes " celebrated its second centennial. The
service brought together from many distant localities the descendants of the original communicants, eager to show their reverence for this
visible link between the flourishing city of Wilmington and the past.

In the churchyard lie the dead of many gen-
erations, of almost every religious denomination.
Here, with the Swedish colonists who came to
America early in the seventeenth century, lies
the late Bishop Alfred Lee of the Episcopal
Church. Although most modest in his demean-

our and his pretensions, so ripe was his judgment and so intimate his knowledge of the Holy Scriptures that he was selected as a member of the American Committee for the Revision of the King James Bible. In the old Trinity grave-yard, too, lie the remains of the Hon. Thomas F. Bayard, who won for himself and for our government such high esteem and praise during his ambassadorship at the Court of St. James's, to which he was appointed by President Cleveland.

KING'S CHAPEL

BOSTON, MASSACHUSETTS

O N Tremont Street, one of Boston's busiest thoroughfares, stands King's Chapel, the first edifice of the Protestant Episcopal Church in New England, at the laying of whose corner stone in 1749 Governor Flurley of the Massachusetts Colony acted as master of ceremonies.

The organisation of the parish dates from May 15, 1686, when the British frigate *Rose* brought to Boston the Reverend Robert Ratcliffe, an established minister of the Church of England, together with the members of a commission appointed by King James II. to preside over the Church in America.

Soon after the arrival of these dignitaries they asked permission of the three congregations then owning houses of worship in Boston to use their church for service, a request which met with a curt refusal. At last permission was grudgingly given for the use of a large room in the east end of the town house, which occupied the site of the present City Hall. This offer of an

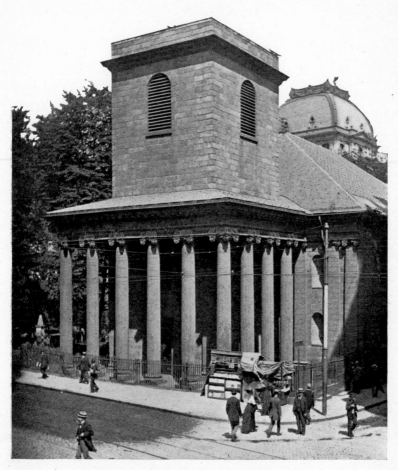

King's Chapel, Boston, Massachusetts

unconsecrated building failed to meet the appro-
bation of those in authority in the Colony, and
on March 2, 1687, the new Governor, Sir Edmund Andros, sent a peremptory order to the
trustees of Old South Church to throw open
their edifice for Episcopal service. A committee
from this church called upon the Governor and
informed him that their church property did not
belong to the state, but to their individual organisation, and declined to accede to his demand.

Two days later, on Good Friday, the Governor ordered the sexton of South Church to
throw open the doors forthwith and ring the bell
to summon people to worship. With fear and
trembling the sexton complied and the Governor with his staff attended service. Before the
recall of Governor Andros in 1690, a small
chapel was built, but as to how the land was procured or when the building was consecrated, no
records tell us. Some little description is ob-
tainable of the building, however, which was
square in form, with a square tower at the west
end, while from the roof rose a staff supporting
a weather vane with an English crown just
below it. This is said to have been the fifth
house of worship erected in Boston.

When the news of the death of King James
II. of England reached America in 1702 the
little Episcopal chapel was draped in mourning.
It had never been named, and to celebrate the

accession to the throne of Queen Anne it was
called Queen's Chapel.   King James II. had
sent to the little chapel the Bible that is still in
use in the church, together with a valuable silver
communion service.   Queen Anne sent over a
red silk damask cushion for the pulpit, surplices
for the rectors and choir, and linen for the altar.
The communion rail was also a gift from England.   Some years later a clock, presented to
" King's Chapel " by " gentlemen of the British
Society " in Boston, was placed in position with
considerable ceremony.

At the Easter service in 1703 a meeting was
announced for Whit-Sunday to consider the enlarging of the church building.   A subscription
was raised and the work begun in 1710.   The
chapel was practically rebuilt, being enlarged to
twice its former size.   More than three years
were occupied in this work.   In the remodelling
of the interior the vestry stipulated that each
member should pay the cost of building his own
pew, a method which, since each pew holder con-
sulted his own taste, resulted in a wide diversity
of styles.

Fronting the pulpit were two large, square
pews, one for the family of the rector and the
other for the use of the Governor and his staff,
together with any British officers who might be
stationed in Boston.   Directly behind these were
two long pews, the front one being reserved for

the " Masters of the Vessels," and the one at its back for eight old men of the parish.

The luxurious interior of the church contrasted so noticeably with the rude simplicity of the Puritan meeting-houses that this Episcopal house of worship was regarded as a blot upon the soil of Massachusetts. Its walls were decorated with banners, escutcheons, and coats of arms of the King of England and the Governor of Massachusetts, as well as of the noble families of England whose members occupied pews in King's Chapel. On the east wall were painted the Ten Commandments, the Lord's Prayer and the Creed. The pulpit was of the prevailing style, being small, narrow and raised high aloft above the heads of the congregation. On it stood an hourglass in an elaborate brass stand. When the chapel was reconstructed in 1710-13 the pulpit was moved to the "next pillar at the easte, near the centre of the church."

In 1741 it was decided that the little chapel was no longer big enough to accommodate the parish, and a committee, of which Peter Faneuil was treasurer, was appointed to secure subscriptions for a new church. By March, 1753, it was found that King's Chapel was in too bad repair for further use, and next month it was demolished. The new building, whose corner stone was laid by Governor Flurley in 1749, was not quite ready for occupancy and the parish worshipped in the meantime with the members of Trinity Parish in their church edifice.

An organ purchased in Europe by subscriptions from members of the parish, and said to have been selected by Händel, was installed in the new church in 1756. In 1772, through the influence of Governor Hutchinson, King George III. presented to the parish an additional eucharistic service of silver, and a new pulpit as well. King's Chapel was regarded as the protégé of the English royal family, and became the favourite place of worship among the officers of the British army in Massachusetts.

While the Continental troops occupied Boston during the Revolution, King's Chapel was closed. When it was again opened for worship, the parish extended an invitation to the Old South Church to occupy it until necessary repairs could be made to their own edifice, which had been desolated by the British army. The Old South Church members accepted the offer and gathered in King's Chapel for worship for nearly five years.

In 1790 a colonnade was added to the west end, or front, of the church building; the crown and mitre were removed, and the Governor's pew with its elaborate hangings gave place to two simple pews of a smaller size. Except for these alterations the interior of the building remains as it was when Boston society and the rank and

file of the British army worshipped in it. The
exterior has seen no change since 1790. The
colonial feeling of bitterness against King's
Chapel on the part of other denominations sub-
sided gradually, and disappeared entirely when
the parishioners offered their church so promptly
to the members of the Old South.

THE FIRST PRESBYTERIAN CHURCH

ELIZABETH, NEW JERSEY

THE church organised by the Presbyterian settlers of Elizabeth, New Jersey, enjoys the distinction of being the oldest English-speaking church within the boundaries of the State. Its first church building was begun by the settlers of Elizabeth two years after the necessary organisation was effected in 1664, a commodious and substantially-built structure that was in excellent condition at the time of the Revolution—more than one hundred years later. In 1760 an addition measuring some twenty-four feet was made to the original building. A gallery was also built, and a high steeple, in which were placed the church bell and the town clock.

There lived no more ardent adherent to the cause of the Revolution than the pastor of this First church, the Reverend James Caldwell, who performed also the duties of chaplain to the New Jersey regiments. His popularity among both officers and men was unbounded and enabled him to do valiant work for the Master among all classes. He stood high in the confidence of General Washington, and was responsible by his hope and courage for much of the reaction from the despondency that for a time prevailed as to the final result of the war. Of him Washington said, " No man in New Jersey has contributed so much toward giving direction and energy to the thoughts and movements of her citizens."

During the Revolution the church at Elizabeth became more or less of a centre around which many skirmishes and engagements took place between the contending armies. In the course of one of these fights the Reverend Mr. Caldwell, finding that the rounds of wadding were running short, hastily brought from the church copies of the hymn books and tearing out leaves distributed them to the men, to be made into wads for their guns, exclaiming: " Give them Watts, boys! Give them Watts!"

The church also served the Continental army as a hospital for the sick and wounded, and gave its steeple as a watch tower, its bell sounding the first alarm of an advance of the British.

With a pastor and congregation so united and energetic in the cause of freedom, it is not remarkable that opportunity for vengeance should have been sought by the enemy. On January 25, 1780, the church was fired by an emissary from the British ranks and utterly destroyed.

Not content with this, the English succeeded in killing both the pastor and his wife, first one and then the other being shot in ambush. They left behind them six children, who were cared for tenderly by the congregation. The last resting place of this " fighting parson " and his wife is the graveyard about the church they both loved so well, where they did such noble work for both their country and their God.

For several years after the destruction of their church the Presbyterians worshipped in a large storehouse temporarily fitted up for the purpose. The war had left many of them almost ruined financially, but soon after peace was established and their finances improved, the subject of building a new house of worship was taken up with vigour. So earnest were the members in their determination to build a new church that funds were not found lacking, and by 1791 the congregation was again housed. The present building still in use, and the centre of many endearing reminiscences, is the structure then raised, and, occupying the site of the original church, is one of the most interesting objects to all visitors to Elizabeth.

ZION REFORMED CHURCH

ALLENTOWN, PENNSYLVANIA

THE earliest settlers in and about Allentown, Pennsylvania, came from Switzerland or the Palatinate, and were members of the Reformed faith. Hence, the earlier history of Zion Reformed Church is largely identified with that of Allentown. Indeed in the same year that the town was founded, 1762, the founders built a log house for a place of worship, using it also as a schoolhouse for many years. The present church stands just in the rear of the site whereon this log house was erected.

The congregation early showed great wisdom in the selection of pastors who should, in serving them, advance also the cause of the church in that part of Pennsylvania, and from the beginning prospered well. In 1770, by permission of Governor Penn, there was a goodly collection of funds for the erection of a new church building, and two years later, on June 25th, the corner stone for this second church was laid. The new church was built of stone, at the then considerable cost of about fifteen hundred dollars.

Some years later, during the Revolution, the church served as sanctuary and place of refuge for the famous liberty bell. When the British occupation of Philadelphia became inevitable there was great fear lest the bells of Christ Church, and the "Liberty Bell" in Independence Hall, might fall into the hands of the enemy and be melted into cannon. To avert this fate, made probable by the number of Tories in the city, some of the patriots of the town, keeping their own counsel, quietly loaded the bells on waggons and hauled them from the city up into the mountain districts where loyalty was unquestioned. When they reached Bethlehem, with its State hospital for the Continental Army, one of the waggons broke down under its load, but rather than conceal the bells there, the location of the hospital being known to the British, the rescue party urged itself on to Allentown. Here, under the floor of Zion Reformed Church, the bells remained hidden until the War was over.

As the population and wealth of Allentown increased, this old stone church became less suited to the comforts of the larger and more prosperous congregation, which in 1838 laid the corner stone of a more modern structure, and on the 7th and 8th of June, 1840, completed it and dedicated the edifice to the worship of God. Until that time services had been rather inter-

Zion Reformed Church, Allentown, Pennsylvania

mittently held, but from now on the congregation enjoyed a minister of their own, and services were given alternately in the German tongue
of the Fatherland, and in the English of the
new country which the worthy members had
adopted.

ST. ANNE'S PROTESTANT EPISCOPAL CHURCH

BURLINGTON, NEW JERSEY

ON Lady Day, March 28, 1703, the corner stone of the venerable church of St. Anne, in Burlington, New Jersey, was laid by the Reverend Doctor Talbot, the rector of the parish, and the first service was held in it on August 22 of the same year, before the building was finished. The church records show that the first communion celebrated within its walls was upon the following Whitsunday.

The name given to the new parish and church seems to have been a matter of considerable discussion. The first rector spoke of it always as " St. Mary's," in honour of Queen Mary of England, the wife of William of Orange, and many of his parishioners, staunch adherents to the cause of King James II., agreed in regarding his daughter Mary as the rightful sovereign to honour. They would not countenance the name of St. Anne for their parish, since they regarded Queen Anne of England as an interloper and usurper of the throne. As years went by, however, kindly acts on the part of this

worthy lady toward the American branches of
the Church of England, the many attempts she
made to improve their condition, both materially and spiritually, revived the advisability of
giving her name to the parish. Gradually the
parish came to agree on the adoption of the name
of St. Mary Ann, and as the years went by, later
generations inclined to the name of St. Anne
simply, by which name the parish has been known
for at least one hundred and fifty years.

The old church was built in accordance with
the architectural style in vogue two hundred
years ago, and so substantially was it constructed
that it has never shown signs of decay, but
stands, especially to the antiquary and the lover
of the venerable, as one of the ideal points of
interest in Burlington County, New Jersey.

From a little straggling village Burlington
has become a populous city, contemporary with
whose growth the parish of St. Anne's has prospered, numbering among its members many men
and women of influence in that section of the
State.

Since the settlement long ago of the name of
the parish no differences of opinion have arisen
among the parishioners, but a spirit of the
utmost harmony has existed, together with that
shoulder to shoulder effort that produces the
best results in advancing the cause of the Master.

ST. MICHAEL'S

MARBLEHEAD, MASSACHUSETTS

A QUAINT old New England church that enjoys a peculiar harmony with its surroundings is St. Michael's, in Marblehead, Massachusetts, the organisation of which dates back almost two centuries. Its corner stone was laid on September 2, 1714, and to-day the building is still used regularly for divine worship.

Of the thirty-three persons whose names appear as contributors to the original fund of St. Michael's, twenty-nine were sea-captains, who were in the habit of coming to the port on trading trips and no doubt felt the need of the churchly influence to which they were accustomed at home in England. Not only did they supply money themselves, but they brought from England in their ships nearly all of the materials that were to be used in the construction of the church, including a reredos, surmounted by the royal coat of arms, that was esteemed far the handsomest that had yet been brought to America. The pulpit, of old-fashioned wine-glass confor-

St. Michael's, Marblehead, Massachusetts

mation, was placed in the centre of the northern side of the edifice, with a reading desk in front and a huge sounding-board above it. Even so important a personage as the collector of the port of Bristol, in England, some eight years later, presented St. Michael's with a handsome brass chandelier, which still sways from the same point in the ceiling where it was rehung in 1822. One David LaGallais presented a silver communion service to the parish in 1745, the heavy flagon of which, weighing four pounds and bearing a Latin inscription, is still in use.

When the news of the signing of the Declaration of Independence reached Marblehead a mob of patriots broke into St. Michael's, tore down the royal coat of arms from the reredos and rang the old bell for Liberty till it cracked. Services were for a long time suspended, inasmuch as the rector, with many of his flock who were of Loyalist turn of mind, fled to Nova Scotia for safety. They took with them incidentally the highly-prized silver communion service and the parish records. These latter were returned after the close of the war, but the articles of the service, all but the old flagon, never found their way back. During these same troublous times, one churchman of St. Michael's, so greatly did he fear lest in the destructive fury of the mob all copies of the Prayer Book should be burned, distinguished himself by copying with pen and ink the complete contents of the Book of Common Prayer.

In 1786 the chanting of the service was introduced at St. Michael's, at that time an innovation in American Protestant churches.

In the course of time, as one by one the families of the communicants died or removed to distant localities, the parish was so depleted that in 1818 funds were no longer forthcoming for the support of the church. The church building was closed, and the glebe sold to pay off the debt of the parish. In 1833, however, vigorous attempts on the part of the Congregationalists to secure possession of the church edifice roused the whole Episcopal church of the United States, until parish after parish contributed aid and old St. Michael's was once more set upon its feet.

St. Michael's church contains many beautiful memorial windows. One, representing Moses on Mount Sinai, was a gift from the Massachusetts State Senate; another, the gift of Mrs. Thomas Appleton, has for its subject Dorcas distributing garments to the poor. The memorial window presented by the Haskells depicts the Ascension.

The first organ set up in the church was a purchase from old St. Paul's in New York City, an instrument on which the inaugural march was played when George Washington took the oath of office as first President of the United States.

During the great fire at Marblehead in 1877, when all the town seemed doomed to destruction, the old Church was saved only by the most heroic efforts. It still stands, the most noble sort of monument of the past, and the recent addition of a commodious chapel and parish house shows the continuing progressive spirit of its parishioners.

GLORIA DEI

PHILADELPHIA, PENNSYLVANIA

ON June 30 and July 8, 1697, meetings were held by the Swedes who had settled in and about Philadelphia to consult upon the building of a new house of worship in that city. Hitherto they had met in two antiquated structures lying a number of miles apart, one at Wicacoa and the other at Tranhook. Both of these buildings growing more and more dilapidated, it was decided in the July meeting that the two congregations should unite their funds and erect a joint house of God at a point that should be convenient for both. No less than fifty-seven families were represented, their church organisation dating back more than thirty years, to the time of the first Swedish emigrants to America in 1667.

Ground was broken for the new church on September 19, 1697, the site along the Delaware River having been presented to the congregation by Svan Swanson. Work progressed so rapidly that within one year the building was almost ready for consecration. Upon the west end of the church a cross wall was intentionally left unfinished until it could be learned whether a chime of bells could be obtained from Sweden, in which case a belfry was to be added. The church was of ample dimensions, being sixty by thirty feet and twenty feet high. The corners on the eastern side were flat and the foundations were of stone, while the walls were of brick, each brick glazed separately.

The building was dedicated on July 2, 1700, by the pastor, the Reverend Eric Bjork, and in token of the thankfulness of the parishioners it was given the name " Gloria Dei." The Swedes were now joined in worship regularly by many English families, who shared their gratification.

In 1704, when the walls seemed about to give way under the weight of the roof, a sacristy was erected adjoining the north end of the structure and a vestibule built against the south side, over the great entrance door, additions which materially strengthened the walls.

In 1710 permission was granted to members of the Church of England to use Gloria Dei for worship each Sunday after the Swedish service was over with. At this later service, which began at eleven o'clock in the morning, a hymn was invariably sung in Swedish as a token of the unity existing between the two organisations. This harmony, as a matter of fact, naturally paved the way for the gradual adoption of English in the regular services of the church.

The old church is still in use, and upon May 27, 1897, the two hundredth anniversary of the dedication of the building was held, an occasion which brought together many of the descendants of the pioneer members of the parish.

"OLD NORTH"

CHRIST CHURCH

BOSTON, MASSACHUSETTS

THE Old North Church in Boston owes its existence virtually to differences of opinion on the subject of the execution of King Charles I. of England in 1649. So various were the arguments for and against the regicide, ecclesiastical and otherwise, that among other dissensions certain worshippers in the New World seceded from the "First Church" in Boston and established themselves as the "Second Church of Christ," their edifice, on account of its geographic location, becoming known as the North Church. The new organisation avowedly stood for political as well as religious independence, and amply justified its title, conferred upon it by a British officer, of "a nest of traitors."

The new organisation came into being in 1650, but the members were too poor at first to build a house of God, or even to pay for the services of a minister. This last they atoned for later by the repute of their pastors, for their third minister, chosen in 1664, was no less a worthy than the

famous Increase Mather. Under his pastorate
indeed, the church began a career which has, perhaps, been of more influence than that of any
other one church body in America.

The structure in which Increase Mather
preached was a large square building, with a
high pulpit and high-back pews. Some of these
latter had private doors that led out into the side
street. The church was used also as a firehouse,
and on the outside of the building were ladders
for use in case of fire. Like many other early
church interiors, Old North was innocent of
stoves. Ironically enough, in view of these facts,
the church was destroyed by fire in 1673, and
was replaced the following year with a much
larger edifice, also of wood. This building,
which was provided with a low belfry, was regarded as "a model of architecture," and served
as a house of worship for almost one hundred
years, or until the winter of 1775-6, when it was
torn down and used for firewood by the British,
after having been used as a firehouse and public
arsenal for powder by the town corporation.
From the time the original church was built the
duties of the citizens and patriots as well as
Christianity had been preached from its pulpit,
and to the vigorous patriotism of its members
no doubt was due in a great measure the particularly harsh treatment the building received at the
hands of the enemy.

The Old North Church, Boston, Massachusetts

After the close of the Revolution, the Old
North Church united with the " Brick Church,"
whose membership had been greatly reduced, a
formal union of the two bodies being effected
in 1779.

From its foundation much of the name and
fame of this celebrated church has been due to
the personnel of its ministry and members. Increase Mather was known throughout the Colonies and his repute still lingers. The great
Emerson began attendance of divine worship
there in 1829, and by his influence and personal-
ity no doubt roused his fellow members to a
sincere spiritual life. In 1840 began the pastorate of the Reverend Henry Ware, under whom
came about the separation from the orthodox
Congregationalists. The beginnings of the
great American crusade against intemperance
date also from this time. The Reverend Henry
Ware's important influence in ecclesiastical, political and social spheres was thrown in favour
of this new cause, and undoubtedly lent new
glory to Old North.

THE OLD TENNENT CHURCH

FREEHOLD, NEW JERSEY

CLOSE to the battlefield of Monmouth, near Freehold, New Jersey, stands an old church, the original organisation of which was formed by Scotch Covenanters in 1692. A simply constructed meeting-house some five miles north of the present site served as the first church structure. This rudely built house of worship was used for forty years, until in 1731 the congregation erected the present church, which has long been known by the name of its most famous pastor, the Reverend William Tennent, who came to America from Ireland in 1730. The church is built of wood, with a shingle roof, and from the date of its erection has invariably been painted white. During its earlier years it was called the " Scots Church," and its corporate title is " The First Presbyterian Church of the County of Monmouth," but its familiar name is always the Old Tennent Church.

The Old Tennent Church has witnessed many stirring scenes. Within its walls the evangelist Whitefield preached one of his most famous sermons. On June 28, 1778, the Battle of Monmouth was fought around it and Washington made his headquarters in the churchyard, conducting the movements of the army from that point of observation. One of his subalterns, who, while sitting on a tombstone tying his shoestring, was dangerously wounded by a cannon ball, was carried into the church, temporarily a hospital, and to this day the stains of his blood are plainly to be seen on the cushion of the seat where they laid him, as well as upon the floor. The churchyard also contains the graves of many soldiers of both armies, and is the last resting-place of Colonel Monckton of the British army, killed in the Battle of Monmouth.

In 1751 the edifice was rebuilt and enlarged in order to meet the demands of its increased attendance. No change, however, was made in its interior arrangements, and to-day the church used regularly for divine worship is as it was in the days of its infancy. Embowered in a grove of forest trees, in the centre of its graveyard containing more than two thousand graves, it presents a most ancient and venerable appearance. One of the most interesting features of the interior is the facsimile, hanging on its walls, of the handsomely emblazoned Royal Charter granted to the Church organisation by King George II.

ST. GEORGE'S

HEMPSTEAD, LONG ISLAND

IN 1702 the Society for the Propagation of
the Gospel sent out from England the Reverend John Thomas, who held his first
service in Hempstead, Long Island, conducting
it in what was known as the Independent meeting-house. Governor Keith, who had been
reared as a Quaker, in describing this event, declared that "such a multitude of people had
gathered that the church could not hold them;
and many stood outside the door or looked in
through the windows." This was the first Episcopal service ever held on Long Island.

The first Protestant Church in Hempstead,
St. George's, was built in 1704, and on December
26th of that year this same Reverend John
Thomas was installed as first rector of the parish.
The communicants were mostly simple farmers,
not heavily endowed with worldly goods, and
they built their first church inexpensively, following the model of the village churches they
remembered in Old England.

Twenty years later, in 1724, this first church
building was outgrown, and on April 8th the

St. George's, Hempstead, Long Island

parish chose a site for the erection of a new house of worship, which they completed within a year. On St. George's Day, April 28th, 1735, the Lieutenant-Governor of the Colony of New York, George Clark, presented the church with the royal coat of arms, splendidly emblazoned. In his capacity of Secretary of St. George's parish he also presented the new church with a set of altar furniture upholstered in crimson damask. A wealthy invalid from the West Indies who spent his summers in Hempstead contributed a silver baptismal bowl. To these were added from time to time the Bible, the Prayer Book, the pulpit frontal and the original silver communion service that had been given to the little church in 1705 by Queen Anne.

The church edifice was of the usual cruciform type, having round arches and the sides and roof being shingled. Its dimensions were fifty by thirty-six feet, and there was a tower fourteen feet square, surmounted by a steeple one hundred feet high. In the walls of the church near the entrance was a tablet bearing the verse from Ecclesiastes, " Keep thy feet when thou goest into the House of God." There were in all some eighteen pews, the front one deeded to Lieutenant-Governor Clark, who was also one of the vestrymen of the parish. On June 27, 1735, St. George's received its charter from the State of New York.

During the Revolution the sacred building was put to use as a stable by the British troopers stationed in the vicinity, and services were interrupted until after the close of the war, when the energetic and God-fearing parishioners carefully repaired it, brought out their treasures from their hiding places, restored order once more, and again held worship there. On November 3, 1785, the first ordination in the State of New York took place; the candidate for orders was John Lowe from Virginia, and Bishop Seabury officiated.

In 1842 the little church building gave place to a larger and more modern structure, built of all that was available of the old materials, and occupying the same site as its predecessor. This building is still occupied by the parish as a house of worship, and in the little churchyard are graves of British officers and soldiers of both armies side by side with those of former members of the parish. Among these lies the body of the first Protestant Episcopal Bishop in America, the Right Reverend Samuel Seabury, who died in 1764.

TRINITY CHURCH

NEWPORT, RHODE ISLAND

THE history of Trinity Protestant Episcopal Church of Newport, Rhode
Island, is replete with interest. The
date of its organisation reaches back to the latter
part of the seventeenth century, while no less
a personage stood sponsor for it than Sir Edmund Andros, the accredited representative of
King James II. to the New England colonies,
as well as to New York and New Jersey.

With the permission of Governor Andros, Sir
Francis Nicholson, the Lieutenant Governor of
New York, organised the parish of Trinity in
1688, although no church edifice was erected until
1702. When this was completed, the wardens
sent a request to the Lord Bishop of London
for a rector, and the Reverend James Honyman came over with but little delay. In 1709
Queen Anne, who was never inattentive to her
churches in America, gave a bell to be placed in
the tower. In the construction of the building
the services of the famous architect, Peter Har-
rison, were employed, and as a result of his
efforts the little Church of England in New-

port obtained a more artistic house of worship than was usual in the early American colonies. In fact, Trinity Church was considered the finest structure of its time.

In 1729 Trinity received a visit from the celebrated dean of Terry, Ireland, the Reverend George Berkeley, Lord Bishop of Cloyne, and the author of the famous verse beginning, " Westward the course of empire takes its way." During a trip which the dean took to the Bermudas in the interest of education, his vessel encountered a severe storm, was driven out of its course, and finally sailed into Newport harbour on a Sunday morning. The dean dispatched a letter to the rector of Trinity Church, announcing his unexpected arrival. This was delivered to the Reverend Mr. Honyman in the pulpit, and after the missive had been read aloud service was postponed while the congregation went in a body to the pier to welcome the distinguished prelate. Upon the return of the Lord Bishop of Cloyne to England, he sent Trinity Church, as a token of the kindly reception he had met, a fine organ with a massive case capped with a crown and two mitres.

The little parish prospered until the Revolutionary War. In those troublous times many of the parishioners whose sympathies were with the British fled from the country, and the more wanton of the Continental army desecrated the church when they occupied Newport. The lion and the unicorn of the royal family of England were torn from the wall, and carried to one of the batteries, where the soldiers used the escutcheon as a target in gun practice. By some good fortune the crowns upon the weather vane and the organ were overlooked and so escaped destruction.

During the war the services were held irregularly, but after peace had been declared the parish promptly repaired the church and secured a permanent rector again.

But little has been done since in the way of alteration, both within and without the church edifice. The same big high-backed pews, the same pulpit raised high upon its pedestal, and the original sounding-board may still be seen. Services are held regularly, and the parish of Trinity has steadily improved.

ST. ANNE de BEAUPRÉ

QUEBEC

ONE threatening day, of the many forgotten days in the sixteenth century,
a terrific storm broke upon a little
band of simple peasants from Brittany, as their
frail vessel made its way up the St. Lawrence
River. They were seeking a home in the new
country that should leave them safe from religious persecution, and in fear of shipwreck at
the very end of their quest they joined in prayers
to the good St. Anne d'Auray. A vow was
made that if the storm should abate through
her intercession they would build a chapel to
her memory. Spared from the tempest at last,
across a little stream from the present parish of
St. Joachim they landed, and there erected a
simple little wooden chapel, never realising that
they were laying the foundations of a church
whose fame should spread to all corners of the
earth.

As the years passed on, a little village, by
name Petit Cap, sprang up about the chapel,
though the original builders, swept on in the

tide of emigration, are unknown by name to posterity.

Weather and storm finally accomplishing their work with this poor little chapel, in 1660 a pious farmer donated land for a new church edifice, providing only that work should begin at once. A priest came from Quebec to bless the land and the foundations, accompanied by Monsieur d'Aillebout, the Governor of New France, who laid the new corner stone. This second chapel, built of stone, arose close to the site of the original chapel. To it flocked thousands of pilgrims, and the wondrous cures that began to be wrought at this shrine of St. Anne became more and more widely known. Among the earliest pilgrims perhaps the most prominent was the first Roman Catholic Bishop of Quebec, a member of the ancient and very honourable family of the Barons Montmorenci de Laval, who had forsaken family and ambition to go as an humble apostle to the Indians in a primitive New World Mission, and step by step had been advanced by the Church until he became its head in Canada.

The reputation of the little shrine in the mission chapel gradually spread to the Old World, and gained the attention of royalty, notably the mother of the French King Louis XIV., Anne of Austria, then Queen Regent during the minority of her son. In the midst of all the affairs of state that could not be surrendered to Cardinal Richelieu she found time to work with her own hands a chasuble for the priest in charge of the chapel of St. Anne. Ornamented with red, white and black arrows, with a quantity of artistic gold and silver embroidery, this chasuble is still one of the most cherished relics of St. Anne de Beaupré, and at all feast days is placed upon the altar. Bishop Laval also gave a costly silver reliquary, studded with gems, and two pictures painted by a Franciscan friar. A crucifix of solid silver was the gift in 1706 of the great French explorer, Lamoine d'Iberville. In 1775 the Lieutenant Governor of Quebec presented to the church a magnificent banner seven and one-half feet high and four and one-half feet across, with a painting on it representing the good St. Anne and the Virgin Mary. Even more touching than these relics, which can be seen to this day, are the many discarded crutches and other pathetic aids of infirm humanity with which the shrine is stacked. Mingled with these also are hearts of silver or gold, presented as memorials of wondrous cures experienced by the more wealthy of those who have sought aid of the good St. Anne.

A new, and third church, built in 1776 to accommodate the increasing throngs, was blessed and crowned by a rescript from the hand of His Holiness, Pope Pius VI., bearing the date of

May 7th, and declaring St. Anne the patron saint of the Province of Quebec. Within the new church are no less than eight altars, gifts to the parish from active bishops of various provinces of Canada. The Cardinal at Quebec gave the high altar, the parishioners gave two unusually beautiful stained glass windows, which attract universal admiration in the chancel. Upon the walls of the church are many paintings by artists who have depicted their deliverance from shipwreck or other ill fortune.

In order to preserve as much as possible of the original church, the Chapel of the Processions, consecrated October 2, 1878, and in design following the original plans, was built largely out of the original materials. The same tower was used, and the old bell still calls its multitudes of pilgrims. The little chapel stands upon an eminence, and just at the entrance door gushes out a fountain, at which the weary pilgrims quench their thirst. Above this fountain is a statue of Bonne Ste. Anne de Beaupré, the number of whose pilgrims is almost incredible, and annually increases.

THE FIRST DUTCH REFORMED CHURCH

NEW YORK CITY

THE first meetings of the Dutch Reformed Church in New Amsterdam were held in the loft of a horse-mill which the settlers had made shift to fit up with seats and chairs, having provided for this second-story loft when the mill was built as a less costly expedient than the erection of an entire church.

In 1642 the First Dutch Church of St. Nicholas, as the members had styled their organisation, reared its first real house of worship, which was built within the fort, for better protection against the Indians. It was a simple enough thing in architecture, with two peaks in the formation of its roof, between which a "tower loomed aloft," but such as it was accommodated the worshippers till 1691.

At that time in narrow Liberty Street, near by, an old lady, Mother Drisius, who owned an extensive peach orchard, a desirable plot of ground, was induced to sell it to the Dutch Reformed Church of St. Nicholas, and upon this site they erected the building that was dedicated in 1693, by far the most substantial and the finest church yet built in Manhattan. It was a rectangular structure of brick, with a square steeple, so large that its base made a room big enough to accommodate the meetings of the whole consistory. The windows of the church were long and narrow, each containing many small panes of glass upon which Master Gerard Duyckinck burned the coats of arms of the principal families of the congregation. The bell and the pulpit, as well as such other furniture as the original church building had boasted of, were transferred to the new house. Conspicuous among the interior decorations of the new church were the escutcheons painted in vivid colours upon the interior walls, representing, as on the windows, the arms of each family of prominence included in the church organisation.

Special distinction was given the nine trustees of the church, for whom seats directly in front of and below the high pulpit were provided.

In 1694 the members of the Consistory sent to Holland a quantity of silver coins from which was cast the baptismal bowl that has since been used for every St. Nicholas generation. The most skilled silversmiths in Amsterdam were employed to cast and ornament it. The church has long regarded this bowl as its most precious possession, with its engraved sentiments composed by Dominie Selwyn, and its rich associations.

As the years went on and Manhattan village grew, the little church in Liberty Street proved too small for the congregation, and new houses of worship were erected, first at Fifth Avenue and Twenty-first Street, and next the present edifice at Thirty-eighth Street and Madison Avenue. Though not ancient in point of years, St. Nicholas' Church as it stands to-day looks back on a quaint and interesting history, from the time when its nine trustees secured the first charter ever granted to a religious organisation in New Amsterdam.

BRUTON PARISH CHURCH

WILLIAMSBURG, VIRGINIA

UNFORTUNATELY for the historian and the antiquary, the earliest history of Bruton Parish Church, like that of St. David's at Radnor, in Pennsylvania, is lost in obscurity, since the original records of the Virginia colonies, both ecclesiastic and of the State, were destroyed before the year 1632. From such meagre data as can be obtained it appears that in that year there was " laid out and paled in " a section of James City County to be designated as " Middle Plantation," which shortly afterward was renamed " Middle Plantation Parish." In 1644 still another parish was formed in this same county, to which the name of " Harrop Parish " was given, and on April 1, 1648, Harrop Parish united itself with the Middle Plantation Parish, the name then being changed to Middletown Parish. The parish of Marston, formed in York County in 1654, was embodied twenty years later in the parish of Middletown, to which again the parish name of " Bruton " was given. The origin of this new designation may be inferred from the fact that directly at the entrance of the north transept door of the Bruton Parish Church is the tomb of Sir Thomas Ludwell, with an inscription stating that Sir Thomas was born " at Bruton, in the County of Summerset," in England. The date of his death was 1678, and it is to this English knight that Bruton Parish owes its name.

That there was an earlier church edifice than the one referred to in the parish records under date of April 18, 1674, is shown by the fact that mention is definitely made of the " Old Church," as well as of a decision reached by the vestry of Bruton Parish to build a new church, " after the model of the one in Williamsburg." The beginning of a church existence in this building, the foundations of which were unearthed quite recently, is noted in an entry in the parish records under date of November 29, 1683:— " Whereas, ye Brick Church at Middle Plantation is now finished." The first service held in the new edifice was on Epiphany Sunday, 1684. The records also speak of an " old communion table " which had been removed to the rectory, and also of the existence of a " ring of bells."

From the same source we learn that Colonel John Page, to whose liberality the church was indebted for this new edifice, claimed the right to construct for himself and family a pew in the chancel, the other communicants distributing

Bruton Parish Church, Williamsburg, Virginia.

Diocese of Southern Virginia. The foundations and roof timber were renewed and the tower woodwork was restored. The bell presented to the parish in 1761 was replaced in the tower, and a clock which had originally hung in the House of Burgesses was installed there. The high pulpit, with its overhanging sounding-board, again stands in the southeast corner of the church, the chancel occupies its original location, and, with the aisles of the church, is paved with white marble, in which are stones appropriately inscribed to designate the graves that had been so rudely disturbed.

The pews of the church are now arranged in their former colonial style, and over the Governor's pew hangs a silken canopy, while upon the walls of the church has been affixed a tablet commemorating the various Colonial Governors who worshipped in the building. The cost of the restoration has been at least twenty-five thousand dollars, and so deeply is the old Bruton Parish Church imbedded in the affections of the people of Virginia that many years must elapse before there could be any thought of the erection of a new church to supersede the one dedicated in 1715 and still so well preserved.

CHURCH OF THE PILGRIMAGE

PLYMOUTH, MASSACHUSETTS

LIKE many other early churches, the Church of the Pilgrimage in Plymouth formed during the earliest days of the Massachusetts Colony, had an organisation before it could erect a church edifice or support a pastor. The Plymouth Church, for that matter, came into possession of its first house of worship by gift, a benefaction which gave great pleasure and encouragement to the congregation. An old deed gives the North Side Town Square as the site of this original meeting-house.

After the death in 1644 of Elder William Brewster, the first pastor of the Church of the Pilgrimage, its fortunes again reached so low an ebb that the discontinuance of regular services in the little meeting-house was seriously considered. For the next ten years or more there was difficulty in securing and retaining a minister, no one being willing to labour for such a meagre stipend as the congregation felt itself able to offer. The membership of the church in all this time had dwindled down to only forty-seven persons, whose "contributions" could scarcely have formed an imposing aggregate.

ST. DAVID'S

RADNOR, PENNSYLVANIA

FEW churches in this country are of such ancient origin as to be obscure. Such an one, however, is old St. David's at Radnor, Pennsylvania, some sixteen miles from Philadelphia, where it still flourishes.

The first mention of this church in history is as early as 1700, and in that very mention there is a suggestion of a former church built of logs and occupying the site of the present stone building. In this log church, toward the close of the seventeenth century, the settlers garrisoned themselves against an apprehended attack from Indians. A series of Historical Records of Pennsylvania speaks of this " ancient Welsh Episcopal Church, erected of logs, and surrounded by some fifty families," and in a letter written by the Reverend Evan Evans, on behalf of one of the pioneer missionaries of the Society for the Propagation of the Gospel in Foreign Parts, dated June 29, 1719, is a passage in proof of services being held at Radnor once each fortnight from 1700. The old Parish Register, in the possession of the St. David's Church Corporation, also supports these statements. Other letters too are extant, written by this same Reverend Evan Evans, who no doubt was most acceptable to the Welsh settlers in and about Radnor, since he could conduct service in their own language for them.

In 1714 the communicants entered into an agreement with this missionary whereby they obligated themselves to provide a suitable place wherein to worship God. Setting out at once to keep this promise, they obtained possession of a five-acre plot of ground, purchased from a farmer in the vicinity. One says purchased, though no written form of title seems to have been proffered and none ever asked. Singularly enough no litigation has ever arisen regarding the title to the property by the Parish of St. David's, nor any question made of it.

The corner stone of the church was laid May 9, 1715. The building was forty feet long by twenty-seven feet broad, and eighteen in height. According to ancient churchly custom everywhere, it was laid out east and west, with the main door to the south. The eastern wall was pierced by one large window, and two large windows gave light in the north and south walls. The sharp pitch of the roof aided in shedding winter snow or summer rains. An additional door opened into the west wall, but was after-

St. David's, Radnor, Pennsylvania

ward closed up. The windows were pointed, in the Gothic style.

The interior of the church remained unfinished for many years, and being open to the roof exposed the shingles and the marks of the pioneers' axes upon the rafters. No provision was made for heating the church, nor even for seating the congregation, and for forty years there was no flooring save that provided by Mother Earth. Some idea of the scanty furnishing of the old church may be gathered from an account of a robbery that took place in 1740, in which we find mentioned " the breaking open of a chest bound round with iron hoops and the following goods stole out of the same;—one large folio Bible; one quarto Bible; one black gown made of fine Spanish cloth; one chalice; two plates and one basin, being stamped Radnor Church." These vessels, it seems, were highly prized beyond their intrinsic worth, since they were a gift to the parish from Queen Anne herself. Fortunately the opportunities for thieves to escape with their plunder were not many in those days, and the " goods " were all easily recovered.

In March, 1765, the church got its floor, and two years later its vestry house, built on the site of the present Sunday school building. In 1771, under the guidance and inspiration of the father of General Anthony Wayne, a gallery was built around three sides of the interior.

Pews were put in, and rented out in order to secure the parish a more ample income. Many of these pews were erected by private gentlemen for the use of themselves and their families, the head of the household actually taking title to a certain piece of ground within the church walls and constructing his pew in accordance with his own ideas of architecture. Others were erected by the vestry and rented for the support of the church.

At the outbreak of the Revolution, the rector, a loyalist Englishman, declared his intention of continuing to use the liturgy for the King and the Royal Family, but as he had other than Englishmen as a majority among his parishioners he was prevented by bodily force from conducting service for a succession of Sabbaths. He gave in his resignation in May, 1776, and it was promptly accepted. The withdrawal of this Reverend Mr. Currie under these troublous circumstances marks an important change in the church's policy. While the War of the Revolution lasted, no services were held in St. David's, and soldiers from one side or the other alternately made the little stone church their rendezvous and used it for divers ends. The Continental army, camped in the neighbourhood, cut out the lead of the diamond-shaped window panes and moulded it into bullets. They even laid hands on the communion service that had been cherished so religiously. The English too had their use of the church premises, for after the Battle of the Brandywine no less than sixteen British soldiers were interred in the little graveyard of St. David's.

Not until the close of the War, when peace had been fully established, was regular service resumed. One rector served St. David's conjointly with St. Peter's in the Great Valley, St. James' Church at Perkiomen, and the Swedes' Church near Norristown. The selection of this first common rector was made by the congregation itself, without the intervention of the vestry.

Between the years 1809 and 1815 decided improvements took place in and about St. David's. There was a rebuilding and a rearranging of the seats, though the high, straight backs were retained. The old walls around the graveyard were repaired and widened out so as to take in a larger plot of ground. This outward improvement no doubt owed its origin to the ceremony of removing to the graveyard the remains of "Mad Anthony Wayne" in 1809, which brought to St. David's a large concourse of men prominent in national affairs, and opened the eyes of the parishioners to the unkempt condition of their God's Acre.

On July 30, 1820, occurred the first confirmation service mentioned in the church records. At Christmas time of this same year the pretty cus-

tom of decorating the old church with ever-
greens had its origin, and within the next few
years the holding of " Convocations" was instituted.   In 1830 a portion of the long gallery
was removed, the high backs were taken from the
pews, and the arrangement of these so altered
that all pews faced the pulpit.   At the same time
the pulpit was placed in a newly built chancel,
and the huge sounding-board that had hung over
it for so many years was taken down. The hook
on which this board had been suspended for generations is still visible in the rafters. A new parish building was also erected. Only a few minor
changes, however, have taken place in the interior of the old church, such as more modern
arrangements for lighting and an enlargement
of the chancel to accommodate more than one
clergyman.   In the main, old St. David's remains unaltered—a precious heritage to those
who have worshipped within its walls.

THE OLD DUTCH CHURCH

ALBANY, NEW YORK

THE first building occupied by the Dutch Church in Albany, New York, was erected soon after the organisation of the church body in 1652. No description now exists regarding the nature of this first building, but the old pulpit, sent over from Holland, although no longer used, remains as a memento of it. The second church building was erected in 1655 on the same site as that of the first one and before long, the congregation increasing, plans were made for the erection of a third and still more commodious building of stone. Its foundations were laid around those of the old churches, and the walls were carried up and enclosed before the old church—that is, the second church—was disturbed. As a result, only four weeks elapsed between the last service held in the old building and the first exercises in the new.

This third church, built in 1715, rejoiced in a pyramidal roof, a belfry, and a gaily painted and ornamented interior. The new pulpit, in actual use, was octagonal, made of Dutch oak so dark as to resemble black walnut, and richly varnished and polished, while on the pulpit bracket stood the hourglass to time the services strictly. The ceiling and front of the gallery were painted sky blue. Low galleries surrounded three sides of the interior, and a bell rope hung down from the roof into the middle aisle, when not in use being wound around a post planted for the purpose in the centre of the church. At eight o'clock every evening the sexton of the church rang the bell, notifying the residents of Albany that supper time had arrived—a sort of curfew that is still followed in old-time communities.

The windows in the church were richly decorated with stained glass, displaying the coats of arms of the eminent families in the church, among them the Van Rensselaers. The pews occupying the ground floor were assigned to the female portion of the congregation; the men sat in the galleries. Three pews in front, however, were specially reserved, one for the Governor of the State, a second for court officials, and a third for aged and crippled men of the congregation.

In winter the women used hot bricks or portable stoves filled with live hickory coals taken from huge Dutch fireplaces, to keep their feet warm, and it was no unusual sight to see fifty or seventy-five coloured slaves waiting at the church doors to relieve their mistresses of this paraphernalia after services. The men sat with their hats on and carried muffs. When stoves did come in, about 1800, they were placed on raised platforms as high as the level of the gallery, from which bridges ran across to the stove platforms to permit the sexton to attend to the fires. Wood was, of course, the fuel, and since the church had no flooring the ashes were permitted simply to fall to the ground below.

In the midst of the dominie's sermon every Sunday, the deacons would rise, each with a long pole upon the end of which was attached a little bag somewhat like a shrimp net, and begin to take up the collection. To these little bags were attached small bells whose tinkling was supposed to arouse any sleeper, and prevent him from making his drowsiness an excuse for not contributing his mite to the poor. After the collection had been taken the dominie would again resume his discourse—a manner of offertory which prevailed till 1795.

In 1786 so many of the congregation had adopted the English language that the question of holding services in that tongue was agitated; the conservative element naturally opposed the change, and the matter was compromised by adopting English at one service each Sabbath and Dutch at the other.

In 1806 this quaint old church was demolished, and the stone used in the construction of the building which is still occupied regularly each Sunday by the Second Dutch Reformed Church in Albany to-day.

FIRST CHURCH

HARTFORD, CONNECTICUT

IN 1632 there came to Cambridge, Massachusetts, a band of refugees from England, seeking a home in the New World where they might enjoy the same religious freedom that their predecessors, the Puritans, had sought before them. They built a small meeting house in Cambridge, but grew dissatisfied with their surroundings before long, and four years later started west and south through the trackless forest, to seek a country of their own. Most of these pilgrims travelled on foot, driving their cattle before them, and carrying the wife of their leader, an invalid, on a rude litter. They halted and settled down, at the spot where Hartford, Connecticut, now stands, and presently built a little meeting-house, with a thatched roof and of rude but substantial construction.

The removal of these settlers to Connecticut was vigorously opposed by the Massachusetts authorities, who still held them to be subjects of the Mother Church. The Dutch in New Amsterdam equally took offence at this first effort at "Expansion," while daily the new colonists

First Church, Hartford, Connecticut

were in danger of their lives from hostile Indians. To provide better defences against these latter, the settlers of Hartford, Windsor and Wethersfield met in compliance with the request of the Reverend Thomas Hooker, the pastor of the little Hartford flock and one of the most remarkable of men. Each of the three societies represented was heartily in accord in hatred of foreign domination; each sought to worship God in accordance with the dictates of their own consciences, and they met gladly to make joint provision for their spiritual and bodily well-being.

The broad mind of the Reverend Thomas Hooker grasped the true idea of separation between church and state, though it had not yet been promulgated in either the New or the Old World, and under his guidance in that little meeting-house of the First Church of Hartford, Connecticut, occurred the first and original "declaration of independence" ever signed in America. It was indeed one of the first written Constitutions, a remarkable document, which declared the colonists of Hartford, Windsor and Wethersfield independent of all authority save that of God. By implication, independence from Massachusetts authority was meant, though no mention was made of any individual sovereignty. No restrictions were made regarding suffrage on civic questions, as was the case in all the Massachusetts settlements, but each

man was regarded as endowed by his Creator
with inalienable rights—the right to life, liberty
and the pursuit of happiness.

So broad and liberal-minded was the platform
of these "Fundamental Orders of Connecticut,"
as the document was called, that it withstood all
attempts at overthrow, and was indeed the solid
foundation upon which later the Constitution of
the State was raised. When the building for
the little First Church of Hartford was built in
1638, this same leader, Mr. Hooker, had declared
that "the foundation of authority is laid first
by the free consent of the people," and so it was.

Many of the oldest records of this meeting-
house have been destroyed, and therefore much
of its early history is lost to us. That in the
construction of the third church edifice slave labour was employed is one of the items gleaned
from one source or another. This third structure, which was dedicated December 30, 1739,
had many innovations, such as weights in the
windows and fine window hangings. These and
the gorgeous wainscoting must have contrasted
oddly with the utter lack of stoves, and the old-
time hourglass in its place on a bracket beside
the pulpit.

Directly in front of the high pulpit and below
it stood the "Deacon's Table." No contribution box was passed to "take up the collection,"
but instead the members of the congregation

filed in front of this Deacon's Table, placing in its box their individual contributions. Unlike other New England churches, there was no allowance made in the rulings of the church for the selection by the rich or powerful of the better seats in the meeting-house. Everybody lived up to the doctrine preached by the Reverend Thomas Hooker, that in the sight of God "all men were equal."

In 1767 the church was struck by lightning while services were being held. One young woman was killed, and a number of the members were badly injured. Lightning rods, or "protectors" as they were called, were then provided, in spite of many adverse comments regarding this exceeding lack of trust in Providence.

In 1807 the present edifice was erected, and provision was made for the use of stoves. So many of the conservative members of the congregation still carried their "foot-stoves" to church that finally an order was officially given that any foot-stoves found lighted in the meeting-house after service had begun should be carried out by the sexton.

The influence of the little First Church of Hartford was more far-reaching than that of any other church within the boundaries of Connecticut. The early adoption of the platform of perfect equality was remarkable; had Thomas Hooker proclaimed in old England so boldly his

belief that the " privileges of election belonged
to the people " he might have been burned at
the stake, his church itself supplying the fag-
gots.   Equally remarkable is the fact that all
the rights then claimed were granted in a charter
given by Charles I.   It was this famous charter
that so mysteriously disappeared in Hartford
when demanded by the Governor of the State,
Sir Edmund Andros.

CATEDRAL de la VIRGEN MARÍA de la CONCEPCION

HAVANA, CUBA

THE cathedral in Havana to which the remains of Christopher Columbus were brought almost three hundred years after his death in Valladolid, Spain, in 1506, deserves an honoured place among the churches of America.

The Catedral de la Virgen María de la Concepcion was erected in 1724. It is a large, quaint structure with a pillared front, a tower at each angle, and a crumbly, moss-grown surface. It is not beautiful, either from an architectural or an æsthetic standpoint, and could scarcely be called imposing were it not for its age and the spiritual grandeur which surrounds it. The edifice that for more than a hundred years sheltered the remains of the Great Discoverer rather possesses a moral association than any majesty of architecture. The interior nevertheless is finer than the outward appearance would lead a visitor to expect. The lofty dome and the vaulted roof are supported by tall pillars of marble and there is some fine masonry in divers colours, although the dominant hue is a sunny yellow. The walls are covered with rich frescoes whose colouring has been somewhat dimmed by time.

The floor is of variegated marble and is unencumbered by seats, the worshippers kneeling in the body of the church. The high altar is a magnificent piece of workmanship, consisting of a base of various kinds of marble harmoniously blended, and supporting a dome and pillars of porphyry, under which is a statue commemorative of the Immaculate Conception. Behind the altar is the bishop's throne, and here and there around the walls are confessionals with appropriate pictures.

The side altars are of solid mahogany, the ancient " Spanish wood," richly carved and gilded, and there are some fine paintings by old Spanish masters, some of them used as altar pieces. One of these is said to be a genuine Murillo. Among other objects of art carefully preserved by the church is a painting on glass said to have been painted in Italy about the middle of the fifteenth century, and to have been blessed by Pope Sixtus IV.

A mural tablet in the choir on the left of the high altar indicates the place where the bones of Columbus long rested after their various journeyings to and from Spain. This tablet is of pure white marble, most sacredly preserved, and bears in high relief a bust of the great Genoese,

with nautical instruments grouped beneath it.
Below these is an inscription, which translated
literally reads:

> "O remains and image of the great Colon,
>   Endure for a thousand ages, guarded in this urn
>   And in the remembrance of our nation."

Unfortunately for a wish so mightily expressed, the bones of Columbus, doomed as they
were to wandering, were permitted to rest within
the walls of the Catedral de la Virgen María de
la Concepcion for only a little more than a century. They were removed to Spain in 1898,
after Cuba had obtained her freedom from
Spanish rule.

CHRIST CHURCH

ALEXANDRIA, VIRGINIA

ALTHOUGH the number of churches in which the Father of His Country is said to have worshipped, and of pews which he is said to have occupied, seems without end, yet the fact remains that in the building of Christ Church in Alexandria he was actually and intensely interested, and gave liberally to its building fund. In the earlier days in Virginia houses of worship were few and far between. It was not until 1765 that it was found expedient to create the parish of Fairfax, of which, for the next five years, George Washington was an active vestryman. Money was not plentiful, and in order to secure funds for the erection of the church the vestry was obliged to impose upon the parish a tax of some thirty-one thousand pounds of tobacco, by the sale of which the church was built.

The site chosen was at the head of Cameron Street, on a plot shaded by forest trees, an ideal spot to set aside as God's acre. The architect who drew the plans for the building was of the

Christ Church, Alexandria, Virginia

family of the great Sir Christopher Wren, whose wonderful cathedral of St. Paul's in London had already given him an immortal fame. The contract for the erection of the new church was assigned in 1767, the sum agreed upon being about three thousand dollars—a large sum of money at that time. Five years later, from some cause now inexplicable, the contractor had failed to make good his promise, and Colonel John Carlyle agreed to complete the building for an additional one thousand and seventy dollars. One year later, on February 27, 1773, he delivered the church into the hands of the vestrymen, completed. On that same day George Washington purchased for himself and his family a pew, paying almost one hundred dollars for it. He also presented to the church the handsome brass chandelier, with its numerous crystal pendants, that still hangs from the old ceiling.

The completed church was a handsome building in the simple Colonial style. Built of brick and roofed with shingles of juniper, it still stands to-day—a landmark in Alexandria. Until 1812 it had neither chimney nor stove, footstoves furnishing the only warmth to the undaunted worshippers of those early days.

A study of the church's finances is interesting. The old records show the collection of fines " for killing deer out of season " and for " hunting on the Sabbath," money which was employed in alleviating the condition of the poor, the lame, and the blind, as well as in burying them when they shook off their mortal ills. Choice Oronoko tobacco had played an important part in the raising of funds for the erection of the building, and the clergyman's salary was also paid in the same legal tender. The purchase of land for a rectory, also through tobacco, was made in 1770, the "glebe" embracing some five hundred acres. Three years later the vestry were able to build a rectory, "with a dairy, meat house, barn, stable and corn house."

Although forbidden, in accordance with the times, to take part in public service in the church, women seem to have been in unusually high esteem there, for we find that one Susannah Edwards was chosen the sexton of the church, and performed her duties so faithfully that her successor also was a woman.

Though with the exception of Mount Vernon, no extant building in this country is more closely associated with George Washington, Christ Church has other associations too. In its register is found the record of the baptism and confirmation of General Robert E. Lee. During the great war in which General Lee played so important a part the Federal troops occupied Alexandria, and the church was held by the military authorities. Many of the more prominent communicants fled within the Federal lines, and a large mound in the churchyard to this day marks the resting-place of some thirty-four Confederate soldiers who died in the Federal hospitals in **Alexandria**.

ST. GEORGE'S CHURCH

NEWBURGH, NEW YORK

SCATTERED by fierce religious persecution and beggared in purse, yet with
their religious ardour still unquenched,
aided by good Queen Anne of England, many
Lutherans came to America from the Palatinate.
Though absolute paupers, they were rich in moral
character, and they brought from their home on
the banks of the Rhine a love of liberty, both
political and religious, that planted the germs of
independence in the region about the Hudson
River, and made it, in a moral sense as well as
a physical, the Rhine of America.

The patent granted these humble Lutherans,
known as "the Palatine Parish by Quassaick,"
embraced some forty acres of land for high-
ways and five hundred for a glebe. This was
donated to the First Lutheran Church of Newburgh, and lies to-day in the heart of the city.
The first minister who served this people was the
Reverend Joshua de Kockerthal, who came with
the first band in 1707, and led them through
many vicissitudes until he was called to his
heavenly reward in 1719.

Upon his return from one of his voyages to

Europe in the interests of his flock he brought
with him a bell for the steeple of the church,
whenever they should be so fortunate as to erect
one; this was a gift from Queen Anne and was
most gratefully cherished by her protégés. Their
first church, dedicated in 1730, was about twenty
feet square, without floor or chimney. The roof
slanted up from each of the four sides, and upon
the apex so formed a small cupola was constructed to contain Queen Anne's bell.

The congregation occupied this building until
1747, when many rumours reached the settlement of the excellent farming and fertile soil
of Pennsylvania, and a goodly portion of the
parish migrated to that State. Their successors
and those left behind in attendance at the little
chapel were of English and Scotch descent, and
being in the majority introduced the service of
the Church of England. From July 19, 1747,
for some twenty-five years, the Reverend Heze-
kiah Watkins of the Church of England conducted service regularly in the little church. The
few remaining Lutherans in the community did
not give up without a struggle, but in the end
succumbed, and after considerable trouble between the members of the two organisations, left
the Episcopalians in possession of the edifice.

On July 30, 1770, a charter of incorporation
for St. George's Parish was obtained from King
George III. of England, and all went well till

the Revolution. The troubles of good churchmen at that time were most grievous, since even
the name of "Churchman" became synonymous
in the popular mind with "Tory" or "Loyalist." By the end of the war the communicants
of St. George's were either driven out of the
country, or so reduced financially that they were
powerless to undertake the repairing and reopen-
ing of their little church without assistance from
their more fortunate brethren in other sections
of the State. Happily the church building was
left them, practically unharmed, except for
broken window-panes and other minor injuries,
and in 1790 the parish was able to secure the services of the Reverend G. H. Speirin, who also
taught in the glebe school, in order to get a better living than the meagre purses of the communicants of the parish afforded as rector's
salary. He served the parish for two years,
and after his acceptance of a call to the parish
of Christ Church in Poughkeepsie, no regular
rector served St. George's until 1816. By
that time the parish had recovered from the
financial straits into which the Revolution had
thrown it, and had secured the means to erect
a new church building and instal another
rector. Their choice fell upon the Reverend
John Brown, who ministered to them almost
three score years and ten before he went to
his reward. With his advent into the church

came prosperity. A new church edifice was erected in 1819, and several years later galleries were built around three sides of the building, and an organ was procured. In 1834 the church was materially enlarged, a steeple was added, and a bell hung in the belfry. In 1853 numerous changes were made and the church building was still further enlarged; a Sunday school house was built and a new organ was set up.

With all these enlargements, still the number of communicants increased, and to accommodate them the vestry purchased and fitted up another building, which was consecrated on May 10, 1859, as St. John's Chapel. St. George's Mission was opened in 1873, and a chapel built for it also in 1880. In 1874, the Ladies' Guild undertook the formation of a home and hospital, an enterprise which was carried to a successful issue, the buildings being dedicated on January 5, 1876, under the title of St. Luke's Home and Hospital. In 1880 and 1881 St. George's was remodelled, and the pews made more comfortable and modern; the chancel was decorated and a beautiful window placed in it. Three years later the parish added a rectory to its possessions. A spirit of enterprise has always existed in St. George's, and of interest in the work of the Master, while great harmony prevails among the parishioners, and pride in the church to which they belong.

ST. LUKE'S

SMITHFIELD, VIRGINIA

IN the County of Isle of Wight in Virginia, some ten miles distant from Fortress Monroe, stands one of the most ancient churches of the Old Dominion. It is still surrounded by the stately old trees of the forest, each of them noble in age and nature, far overtopping the Norman tower of old St. Luke's in Smithfield.

St. Luke's was erected in 1632, many well-authenticated records, as well as the imprint in the bricks in the walls, vouching for this date. The east window of the church is composed of no less than seventeen distinct windows, separated from one another by brick mullions. This edifice was used as a house of worship for over two hundred years, when the finances of the parish ran below the expense of keeping the church in repair and maintaining service. Moreover, many of the families of the early parishioners were widely scattered, and the number of communicants was much reduced, until in 1836 the church was finally abandoned. During the following fifty years the old building apparently

St. Luke's, Smithfield, Virginia

fell a prey to relic-hunters, who bore away almost
every removable portion of it, so that when the
Reverend Dr. David Burr, the senior assistant
rector of the Church of the Epiphany at Washington, visited the parish in 1887, scarcely any
portion of the original church remained save the
solid walls.

Thanks to the indefatigable efforts of Dr.
Burr, the restoration of the old building was
undertaken. The pride of native Virginians, especially those residing in Isle of Wight County,
was aroused, and when the restoration was completed the little church at Smithfield enjoyed a
beauty that not only harmonised with its pristine
glory, but in a number of features exceeded any
which the finances of the original parishioners
could possibly have afforded.

Among the new features added were twelve
memorial windows. One was dedicated to the
memory of George Washington; another to that
of General Robert E. Lee, while still others
commemorated the names and deeds of Captain
Bridges, the original builder of the edifice, the
Reverend Mr. Hubbard, the last Colonial rector;
Sir Walter Raleigh; Captain John Smith; John
Rolfe, who married Pocahontas; the first four
Episcopal Bishops of Virginia—Bishops Madison, Moore, Meade, and Johns; while the twelfth
was dedicated to the memory of the Reverend
Dr. Blair, the founder of the College of William

and Mary, the alma mater of President Jefferson and President Monroe.

Not only did the residents of Virginia delight in adding their mites to the restoration fund, but contributions flowed in from people of other denominations as well, and from every section of the country, no less than twenty-one States being represented in the list.

An interesting feature in this work of restoration was the incorporation into the building of some two thousand of the bricks that had been part of the walls of the ancient Colonial church at Jamestown in Virginia years before. The pulpit, as well as the sounding-board, with the carved oak communion table and altar, were memorials from the families of early parishioners who had become residents of Maryland and Pennsylvania. In order to embody in the edifice all that was possible of the original church building in its restoration, the chancel railing was constructed from portions of the original roof, which had finally fallen in.

In short, all the traditions and style of the original structure were carefully followed, and the present church is a most interesting example of early church architecture in the Southern Colonies.

THE REFORMED NETHER DUTCH CHURCH

SCHENECTADY, NEW YORK

ARENT VON CURLEER, who purchased the " Great Flatts " from the
Mohawk chiefs in 1661, is regarded as
the founder of Schenectady. After the deed for
the land had been signed by these Indian chiefs,
he removed to his new possessions in company
with some fifty hardy Dutch pioneers and their
families, forming a little Dutch republic whose
voters were one in their religious belief. The
freeholders in this new settlement constituted
their own official and spiritual authority, and
from their number they elected annually five
trustees for the purpose of " maintaining good
order and advancing their settlement." They
housed themselves promptly in rude log structures and effected their church organisation with
the first election of elders and deacons in 1662.
When in 1664 the government of New York
passed into the hands of the English, both settlement and church government continued placidly
without change.

In the meanwhile the members had been un-

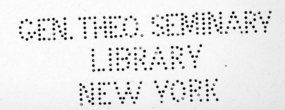

able to support a minister of their own, depending entirely upon travelling missionaries. In 1674, however, they erected their first rude structure and dedicated it to the worship of God. The occasion was one of great rejoicing among the members of the Reformed Nether Dutch Church, since they were no longer compelled, if they desired to attend church service, to travel the twenty miles that lay between themselves and Albany.

This new little church was erected at the south end of Church Street, near the head of Water Street, and was substantially built although utterly devoid of ornament. Neither was much provision made for comfort, since the building had neither flooring nor means of heating. From a lofty pulpit the minister sounded forth his warnings to the congregation, who literally sat at his feet. The building had a gallery which was constructed, not with the idea of providing additional seating capacity, but because from its height a better watch could be kept for attacks by hostile Indians. The windows were high in the walls and built after the manner of the loopholes of a fort.

It was a memorable day in the history of the little community when the Reverend Petrus Thesschenmacher, a graduate of the University of Utrecht, was installed in 1684 as the regular domine of the Schenectady Church; so great

an event in their history that the year 1684 has
ever since been known among them as " the year
of grace." From that year, too, date the regular
appointment of elders and the keeping of the
records of the church. The ordinances and
forms of worship prescribed were considered
rather as privileges than duties and were performed according to the principle that "unto
whomsoever much is given, of him shall much be
required." In consequence, the higher the social
or official standing of an individual, the more
circumspectly was it necessary for him to conduct himself, both in his daily walk and conver-
sation and in his discharge of his religious duties.

Until the installation of this, their first regular
minister, the congregation had received quarterly
visits from the Reverend Gideon Schaets of
Albany, who at these periods baptised and confirmed the young in the Schenectady congregation, administering also the Lord's Supper. Marriage among these pioneers was regarded as a
civil function which the resident magistrate
might perform, according to the ancient Dutch
custom. Upon the installation of the Reverend
Mr. Thesschenmacher a school was also opened,
in which he taught the children of all settlers in
the vicinity; and since the idea of free schools
had not yet been entertained the new minister
was able by means of this tuition to earn the
better part of his living.

In spite of the fact that these humble farmers
had naught but what they earned by the labour
of their own hands, the church as early as 1681
had a fund for the support of the poor amount-
ing to three thousand guilders. To this sum
still another thousand guilders were added by
1690, when the barbarities of King William's
War utterly destroyed the little settlement at
Schenectady, driving the survivors to more
thickly settled portions of New York. The little
Reformed Nether Dutch Church was burned,
and its minister, the Reverend Petrus, mysteriously disappeared and was never seen afterward.

Thoroughly alarmed for the safety of their
families, many of the farmers who had com-
prised the original settlement in and about
Schenectady decided not to return, but to remain in places of greater security. The church
organisation in consequence languished until the
beginning of the next century, when the Reverend Thomas Brower came over from Holland
to make his home among the people of Schenectady. He served the congregation for over a
quarter of a century, and materially increased its
membership. In 1703, almost immediately after
his arrival, another church edifice was erected,
which fulfilled the requirements of the congregation for eighty years, until a new structure
replaced it in 1814. The present church building
was erected in 1862, from plans prepared by a

son of the Right Reverend Horatio Potter, then Bishop of the Diocese of New York.

The present communicants of the church still maintain the same form of church government and the same articles of faith that were so highly cherished by their forefathers when they first came into the wilderness as fur traders in 1661. The only innovation that has been introduced is the adoption at alternate services in the church of the English and the Dutch languages.

SAN CARLOS BORROMEO

MONTEREY, CALIFORNIA

TO write even a skeleton history of the work accomplished by the Spanish missionaries of the Roman Catholic faith would demand several volumes; one can therefore only give a leaf here and there of the methods they employed and the special points they covered.

More than one hundred years before the establishment of any Protestant Church on the eastern shores of our country, there were in existence numerous old Catholic Missions scattered throughout what is now New Mexico, Arizona and California, some of which are in existence to-day.

From Mexico these Jesuit priests travelled, teaching and preaching the gospel of Jesus Christ as they went. Many of them fell victims to hunger and thirst in the deserts, while still others became the prey of wild beasts and savage men. One of those who escaped death entered through the shoals that guard so carefully and hide so skilfully the Bay of Monterey. In

San Carlos Borromeo, Monterey, California.

his little frail boat he sailed up to the head of the bay, landed, and, selecting two stately oaks near the shore, he nailed to them a wooden cross, beneath which he said mass. Later, to provide shelter from inclement weather, a little thatched hut was built close to these oak trees. Journeying on, Gaspar de Portala sought other and more populous sections where he might make converts, finally returning to Mexico, where he made his elaborate report to the Church.

On the missionary, Portala, that journey up the Bay of Monterey made no special impression, and as the years passed on, the exact site of this Bay could not be located. In 1768, however, another member of the Jesuit Brotherhood travelled over the first portion of the route taken by Portala, and by chance entering this same Bay of Monterey sailed to its northern extremity. Here, on landing, he found the two oaks described by Portala, with the wooden cross still nailed to them. Additional evidence of the work of Portala one hundred and sixty-eight years earlier was found in the little thatched hut close to the twin oaks, designating the spot where the standard of Christ was first set up in what is now the State of California. Overjoyed, Padre Junipero Serra, with his followers, knelt in a thanksgiving service beneath the wooden cross, and there it was decided to found the Mission of San Carlos Borromeo on the banks of the Rio

Carmelo. With that ability which the practical turn of his mind gave him, Junipero oversaw and directed every portion of the work of construction of the buildings which were to constitute the first Mission Church in our country. A line of high, strong posts was planted close together, enclosing a rectangular portion of land some seventy by one hundred and thirteen feet; within this a simple log house was erected. For want of nails the outer palisade failed to possess that upper fastening that would naturally bind the poles together at the top and render the enclosure the more secure and durable. To obviate this difficulty Junipero had the inside of the palisade plastered with mud and clay, as well as the walls and roof of the structure erected within the stockade for the use of the missionaries. The building was twenty-one by one hundred and fifty feet in dimensions and divided into seven rooms. One of these was set aside for worship, others as living rooms for the priests and such converts as they might make, while still others were used as a storehouse. Naturally, at first, these remained empty, but Junipero provided for the future material as well as for the spiritual welfare of his neophytes. He taught them the cultivation of the land, and the fruit of this instruction was placed in the storehouses he had provided when the Mission was first founded. The little church was completed, even to the

interior whitewashing, a tedious process at that
time, and the first mass was said within its walls
the day it was dedicated, June 3, 1770. Adjoining the larger structure, a smaller one was soon
after erected to serve as a kitchen, and this, as
well as the large building, was roofed with a
plaster made from mud and clay. This roof did
not prove a success and was soon replaced by
tiles, baked in the little oven that Junipero had
erected for the purpose.

These first simple structures were not intended
as the permanent home of the San Carlos Borromeo Mission, but as accommodations for the
priests, with such converts as they might make,
until more solid, permanent structures could be
raised. The Mission prospered from the very
beginning, and so arduously did all labour that
in December of 1771 the new Mission houses
were completed and occupied. One peculiar
expression which was habitual with Junipero
Serra, and which he invariably used as a greet-
ing, " Amar a Dios "—Love God, was gradually
adopted by the Indians, who would invariably
employ it in accosting the Spaniards. In 1773
Junipero Serra made a report to the Mexican
Church, and it then became known that more
neophytes were being added to the Mission of
San Carlos Borromeo than any other that had
yet been established in our country.

In 1784 Padre Serra was called to lay down

his earthly cross, and his body was laid to rest in the sanctuary of San Carlos.

On July 7, 1792, the corner stone of a new house of worship was laid, and soon afterward, a visit to Monterey of the English voyager, Captain Van Couver, resulted in the gift from this noted explorer of a handsome barrel organ for the use of the Mission.

To the student of architecture, the Mission Church of San Carlos, with its arched western doorway, its central star window, and the severely plain gable is an interesting combination. The most elaborate piece of architectural detail found in any of the Spanish Missions in America is said by an architectural authority to be the ornate clustered columns at San Carlos Borromeo. It is at the entrance to the Chapel of the Sacred Heart of Jesus, and is a reproduction from the Alhambra; showing, no doubt, that the original from which it was evidently copied from memory had been viewed by Padre Serra at some time in his life.

While the founder of the Mission of San Carlos extended his labours into other mission fields, yet the first Mission he founded in California had his deepest love. Here was his home —if a Spanish missionary could be said to possess a home; here, he made his special abiding place. Hence the tower, the star window and the elaborately carved arches, as well as the wealth of carving and painting in the mural decoration. Unfortunately only half obliterated fragments of these remain.

The artistic sense of the founder and builder of San Carlos seems to have exhausted itself in the construction of the Mission structure, and to have left nothing for the furniture. But the altar vessels—the asperger and the candlesticks, together with the baptismal vessels—were rich both in material and workmanship. These are invariably prominently displayed on November 4th, the day of the patron saint of the Mission, after whom it was named, San Carlos Borromeo, that nephew of Pope Pius IV. who died in 1584 and was canonised by Pope Paul V. in 1610. The asperger of San Carlos Mission is a distinctively Moorish design, although naturally of Spanish execution. The handle is cast and turned; the base is hammered from the back, according to the primitive method in vogue in Old Mexico, the design, both in the handle and in the body of the vessel, being an interlacing of moons and rings in arabesque. Among the other highly esteemed possessions of the Mission is the processional cross once borne on feast days by Padre Junipero Serra himself. It is silver chased in a neat and artistic design, both on the front and rear sides. The Christ is of brass and is evidently more modern, having, no doubt, replaced the original figure that must have been lost or stolen during the dark days of the secularisation period. The two altar candlesticks are beautifully ornamented in olive-leaf design.

In 1779 direct communication was established by boat with Mexico, and from that time the Mission enjoyed many years of spiritual and financial prosperity, as the providing of a market for the crops raised on the Mission lands gave a greater incentive to husbandry, as well as to mining.

In 1792 a welcome addition was made to the possessions of the Mission in the form of three sweet-toned bells, which were hung from a heavy framework resting upon a solid stone foundation.

The separation of the church from the state when the territory became American resulted unfavourably for San Carlos Borromeo Mission, and gradually the neophytes scattered; service was held with less regularity, the finances of the Mission grew less and less equal to keeping the building in repair, and finally, in 1852, the roof fell in.

In 1868 prominent Catholics in various sections of California awoke to the fact that the early landmarks of their faith were gradually being lost to history, and a vigorous effort was at once begun to restore many of the mission churches to their former condition, among these being San Carlos. In clearing away the debris preparatory to this work the workmen came across the stone coffin within which lay the skeleton of Padre Junipero Serra, in an inner coffin of redwood. The body was in a state of perfect preservation; even the stole with which he had been adorned at the time of his burial was in excellent condition. The work of restoration continued, and on August 28, 1884, the Mission buildings were again consecrated.

QUEEN ANNE'S CHAPEL

FORT HUNTER, NEW YORK

AT an audience granted to a delegation from America in 1708 Queen Anne promised better protection to the settlers who had colonised the region claimed by the Mohawk and Onondaga Indians. Accordingly, two years later, Robert Hunter sailed for the New World, carrying with him, as the new Governor of New York, royal orders to establish a fort at the junction of the Schoharie and the Mohawk Rivers and to build a church within its walls. The year 1711 witnessed the erection of a fort of logs, well pinioned together. The structure measured twelve feet in height, while the enclosure was about one hundred and fifty feet square, and in the centre of this, and protected by its palisades, rose Queen Anne's Chapel. It was of limestone, twenty-four feet square, and ornamented with a belfry, within which hung the bell, given by Queen Anne to the Mission. Many years afterward this bell was placed in the belfry of an institution of learning at Johnstown, New York, and called the students to their classes until the building was destroyed by fire a few years ago.

The entrance to the chapel faced the north, while the pulpit, capped by a sounding-board, stood on the west side. In the customary position stood the reading desk, and opposite the pulpit were two pews built upon an elevated floor, one for the minister's family, the other for the officer in charge of the garrison. Many years later this officer was the famous Sir William Johnson. Movable seats were provided for the rest of the congregation.

Queen Anne's Chapel boasted the possession of the first church organ west of Albany, a gift from the Queen, as were also the linen for the altar, the cushions for the pulpit and reading desk, the carpet for the floor before the communion table, the pulpit Bible, and three copies of the Book of Common Prayer. The Queen gave also twelve large octavo Bibles for use in the various chapels which she ordered built for the Mohawk and Onondaga Indians, as well as a silver eucharistic set of five pieces, four large shields of Her Majesty's coat of arms for the chapel, three paintings of the Mohawk chapels she contemplated building, and two painted tablets containing the Lord's Prayer, the Creed and the Ten Commandments. As late as the Civil War Queen Anne's brass candelabra with nine sockets, arranged in the form of a triangle (the emblem of the Trinity) and a large cross, still remained in the rectory. The chaplain at the fort, or rectors from St. Peter's at Albany conducted the services in the chapel, adjoining which was a rectory, built in 1712. On November 27, 1741, the chapel received the grant of a tract of land known as Queen Anne's Chapel Glebe, a direct gift from the Crown, and containing some three hundred acres of tillable land.

In spite, however, of this royal munificence, with no settled rector and no permanent congregation, but little care seems to have been taken to keep the chapel in repair, and during the Revolution it suffered in common with all other edifices belonging to the Church of England. The windows were destroyed, the floor was demolished and even the walls were cracked. The silver communion set was only saved by being buried in the Indian reservation of the Mohawks, at the beginning of the Revolution, to be resurrected in 1785 and taken by the Indians under the special guardianship of a daughter of Joseph Brant to the new Mohawk church at Brantford, Ontario, Canada. It is still in the possession of that church, and used on special occasions. Engraved on each piece of plate appears the inscription, "The Gift of Her Majesty Anne, by the Grace of God, of Great Britain, France and Ireland and Her Plantations in North America,

Queen, to Her Indian Chappel of the Mohawks." The Bible remains in good condition to this day and bears on its cover the words, "For Her Majesty's Church of the Mohawks, 1712." Meanwhile the bell still hung in the belfry, but the Mohawks attempted to gain possession of even this interesting relic, and actually secured it and were carrying it away with them in a boat. When the white settlers became aware of the depredation and gave pursuit, the Indians sunk it in the river so hurriedly that they cracked it, but the settlers, nothing daunted, recovered it and hung it once more in the belfry.

The ravages of time gradually threw little Queen Anne's Chapel into dilapidation, and with no churchmen living in the neighbourhood and no services held, it finally became an utter ruin. From the rectory some of the bricks, which had been brought from Holland when the manse was erected, were saved and embodied in the Episcopal Church of St. Ann's at Amsterdam, New York, the church that succeeded to the glebe which had been granted for the maintenance of Queen Anne's Chapel. Of the old chapel not the slightest vestige remains to-day.

DUTCH REFORMED CHURCH

KINGSTON, NEW YORK

AS early as 1659 the Dutch settlers at Kingston, New York, erected with their own hands a little church building, and dedicated it the following year. When a regular minister arrived from Holland this same year he found himself a domine with a membership of but sixteen souls and a salary paid in wheat, which was then legal tender among these humble tillers of the soil.

This first little hand-built house of worship satisfied the needs of the congregation for almost one hundred years, before it was replaced by a more substantial structure, which was dedicated on November 29, 1753. In this second edifice the members worshipped for twenty-five years, when, on October 16, 1777, the church was burned by the British troops that took possession of Kingston under General Vaughan. The British officers were at first half inclined to allow it to stand, as it offered agreeable shelter, but when they learned that its minister, the Reverend Doctor Doll, was one of the most ardent patriots in all New York, they meted out his punishment to him in the form of a fire that destroyed not only his church, but his parsonage too. This parsonage was a stone structure, so carefully built that after both war and fire its walls were employed in the new "Pfarrhaus" that is still standing and regularly occupied.

In 1694 a bell was imported and gave such pleasure to the members of the little parish that they used it to announce the hour for meals for the farmers of the neighbourhood.

The observance of one quaint custom was reminiscent of their former life in Holland— the announcement by the grey-haired sexton, between the ringing of the first and last church bells, that the hour for service had arrived. From door to door he travelled, rapping loudly and crying, " Church time! "

The interior of the church was fitted up in the ancient Dutch style, with a high, narrow pulpit, surmounted by a sounding-board. Notices of all kinds, whether of funerals, christenings, weddings or merry-makings, were handed first to the sexton, who in turn gave them to the clerk, who stuck them on the end of the bamboo pole which he kept for that purpose and reached them up to the domine. At the termination of the service, as in other Dutch churches we have seen, the deacons took up the collection with long poles having little velvet bags hung on the ends and a tinkling bell to wake the sleepers to the responsi-

bilities of a contribution. Money being scarce,
" tokens " stamped by the church were accepted
as coin, though naturally the church expected
them to be duly redeemed. At the communion
service no communicant would think of approach-
ing the table unless suitably attired in black.

The charter of the Kingston Dutch Reformed
Church was granted by the British throne in
1719, and in virtue of that authority the little
Church maintained an independent position, even
when all other churches of its denomination in
this country accepted the jurisdiction of the General Synod of the Dutch Church in America.
In 1818, however, realising that if united with
other churches of its own tenets it could render
greater service in the cause of the Master, it
joined hands with the remaining churches of its
denomination, acquiring representation thereby
in the General Synod.

The little church has steadily prospered and
is still most aggressive in promoting good will
among mankind.

ST. GEORGE'S CHURCH

SCHENECTADY, NEW YORK

QUEEN ANNE'S interest in the American Indians dates from the visit of several chiefs to London during the first decade of the eighteenth century, when they accompanied the Mayor of Albany. The Mayor's mission was to ask additional protection from the inroads of the French throughout the Colony of New York, and pursuant to the instructions of the Queen at this time a missionary was sent out to the Mohawks in 1710. Services were held at stated intervals, the Dutch Reformed Church at Schenectady giving the use of its church building for the purpose. The English settlers, and the Dutch as well, joined with some forty British soldiers stationed at Fort Hunter, regularly attended these services.

In 1731 the Reverend John Miln, who had become rector of St. Peter's Protestant Episcopal Church at Albany, engaged to visit Schenectady four times each year, and to remain with the little parish there five days upon each trip. During one of his earlier visits he appointed the Reverend Henry Barclay lay reader at Fort

Hunter, under whose faithful ministration no
less than five hundred Mohawk Indians were
converted and came regularly to service. Many
of these by 1741 had become communicants in
the little parish, and two years later nearly every
one of the Indian attendants had been confirmed
at some one of the successive visits of the Reverend John Miln. Later, after the terrible mas-
sacres of the French and Indian Wars, during
which settlers in outlying districts abandoned
their farms and fled to Albany for protection,
the number of communicants in Schenectady, of
course, materially decreased.

In 1748 the young clergyman, the Reverend
John N. Brown, came from London to the Mohawk Nation. But twenty-one years of age, he
was full of ardour and entered upon his work
with such energy that he soon convinced the
parishioners they should have the church he
planned for them. In 1759 his hopes were real-
ised and the little church was dedicated as " St.
George's Protestant Episcopal Church." This
same church building is still standing to-day,
although it has been enlarged no less than three
times to accommodate the increasing number of
its communicants.

Sir William Johnson figures among the principal contributors to the fund for the erection of
St. George's. Through the generosity of British officers stationed near Schenectady the church

also acquired a library which was regarded as one of the most valuable outside the City of New York. Unfortunately it was destroyed during the turbulent times of the Revolution, together with the organ and the interior furnishings. St. George's, like other Episcopal churches at that time, fell a prey to the Whigs, and its rector, the Reverend Mr. Doty, barely escaped from the patriot mob with life and limb.

For a number of years after the close of the war the parish could not support a clergyman, and held service irregularly till 1795, when they again called a rector. Since then it has thrived materially and spiritually.

In architecture St. George's resembles the ancient churches of the old country. The original structure was rectangular in shape, fifty feet by thirty-six; its walls, which were built of stone, being three feet in thickness. It was, and is still, divided by two rows of columns of a Tuscan type. Over the nave the ceiling is arched, but flat over the aisles. In order to increase the seating space of the church, a gallery was added later, extending around three sides of the edifice. Later still this was found insufficient also, and transepts were built and a tower was erected against the west end of the church, adding immensely to its appearance. The arched windows are set with coloured glass, with broad mullions.

Within, the pews are of dark red wood, and possess individual doors. The addition of the transepts made an enlargement of the chancel possible, and the galleries, with the exception of the one in the west end above the entrance, were removed.

In 1905, soon after his installation as rector of St. George's, the Reverend Dr. B. W. R. Taylor, the present incumbent, urged upon the vestry a thorough repairing of the church edifice, and through his efforts brought about the complete restoration of the building. Among other presents which the parish received at this time were a new pulpit, a baptismal font, and a lectern, all harmonising in design and material with the pews and interior decorations. In deference to the wish of the Reverend Dr. Taylor, the original white of the interior was restored, and its beauty much enhanced. The charm of the exterior still arouses the interest of all beholders, who often echo the expressions of pleasure that George Washington is said to have uttered when he first viewed old St. George's at Schenectady.

THE QUAKER MEETING HOUSE

FLUSHING, NEW YORK

IN 1692 the Friends were the only religious denomination in Flushing, Long Island, that held regular services, though they had not yet built any church and met only in private houses. During that same year they succeeded in obtaining funds with which to purchase land and erect a meeting-house, and chose three acres of land in what seemed to them a desirable location. On September 3, 1693, they promptly began the cutting of the timber so that they might have a roof to worship under by the following January. The building took a longer time than they had contemplated, and the first meeting was not held in their house of worship until August 4, 1694; the meeting-house was small and plain; it wholly lacked flooring and all means of heating, but such as it was, in two years it was ready for occupancy and the first "yearly meeting" was held in it.

By 1704 it was found necessary to make repairs, and the meeting-house received a new shingled roof, while the walls were replastered.

In this building in 1716 was held the first public
meeting in New York to agitate the abolition of
slavery. The subject was debated also in each
of the ensuing yearly meetings, and in 1718 Mr.
William Burling published an anti-slavery address which had been made before the annual
meeting of the Friends in the Flushing meeting-
house. This was the first anti-slavery publication
ever issued in this country.

In 1716 it became necessary to build a larger
and more substantial meeting-house, and on September 28, 1719, the Friends found themselves
in a new house of worship. This building is the
one now used by the Friends in Flushing and
has undergone few alterations. Originally a
gallery extended around three sides of it, but in
1763 this was removed and a second story added.
This upper story was divided and in one portion
a school was kept for children of the Friends'
families. Three years before this alteration was
made stoves were introduced into the building.

During the War of the Revolution, while the
Friends were holding a meeting one Sunday in
1776, officers of the British Army broke into
the meeting-house and would have seized it, but
were so impressed by the earnest spirit of the
Friends that they agreed to wait until the meeting was over before taking possession. Take it
they did, however, and used it as a hospital, the
divided upper portion serving as a prison bar-

The Quaker Meeting-house, Flushing, Long Island

racks and storehouse for firearms, the fence around the graveyard for fuel.

Many of the Friends suffered from fines, both from the British and from the Colonial Government, because they would not contribute funds for the support of the two armies, but persisted in their worship. While their meeting-house was occupied by the military authorities, they still met in private houses or in barns, no attempts being made, to the credit of the British be it said, to molest the attendants at any of these services.

After the close of the war the meeting-house was thoroughly repaired, and in 1783 was again opened for service. Since that time the Friends have gathered regularly in it and the old house of worship has become one of the quaintest landmarks of Long Island.

ST. ANN'S CHURCH

BROOKLYN, NEW YORK

THE first Episcopal Church in what now constitutes Kings County, Long Island, was established in 1784, soon after the close of the Revolution. It scarcely took the form of a church organisation; the very few Episcopalians in and about Brooklyn being served occasionally by some of the clergymen of New York City, assembling in an upper room in an old one-and-a-half story brick house at No. 40 "Old Ferry Road." No record exists to show that this little band of worshippers was ever incorporated as a church organisation or had any regular officers.

Two years later, however, the first regularly established and incorporated Episcopal church in Kings County was formed; it numbered not more than fifteen or sixteen parishioners, and naturally hesitated about incurring the expense of building a church edifice. The parish hired for worship an old long one-story house at the northwest corner of Fulton and Middagh streets; the interior partitions were removed and a pulpit and seats " with backs " were constructed. These pews were sold later to aid in paying the salary of the first rector of the church—the Reverend Mr. Wright. The parish does not seem to have had any name at this time.

This little humble structure was occupied by the church for more than a year, and in 1787 Mr. John Carpenter transferred to the "Episcopal Church of Brooklyn" a church edifice that had been erected in Fulton Street for a congregation of "Independents." On April 23, 1787, the church was legally incorporated. Through some misunderstanding the right to own the property of the parish was vested in seven trustees. This being contrary to the policy of the Episcopal Church, a reorganisation was decided upon, and the Church newly incorporated, June 22, 1795, under the title of St. Ann's Church, and placed regularly under the government of church wardens and vestrymen.

The Church on Fulton Street, which was surrounded by a graveyard that is still used, was occupied by the parish nearly twenty years, when there was erected a more substantial edifice than the old frame building that had been occupied so long. This new church, built of stone, and larger in proportions than its predecessors, was built on Sands Street. It was dedicated in 1805, and five years later there was installed in it the first church organ used in King's County.

The parish of St. Ann's prospered spiritually

and temporally, and it was found necessary in 1825 to provide for a still larger congregation. A new church edifice, of brick, was built on Washington Street, in close proximity to the older structure. This was consecrated during the latter part of the summer of 1825 by the Right Reverend John Cross, Bishop of New Jersey, assisted by the Bishops of Pennsylvania and Rhode Island. Within its walls were still held the only Episcopal church services in the County of Kings, except those conducted in the chapel of the Navy Yard.

The same spirit of progress is noted in the conduct of the affairs of the parish as have characterised it from the outset. To-day St. Ann's Church is able to boast the only female choir in Brooklyn, while equal care is exercised in promoting athletic sports among the young men of the parish and a spirit of sociability among all, resulting in strong bonds of good fellowship and producing a "home feeling" that is shared with all strangers within her gates.

DUTCH REFORMED CHURCH

NEWTOWN, LONG ISLAND

OF the Dutch Reformed families in early New York many removed from time to time beyond the limits of New Amsterdam, securing for themselves broader sections of land for tillage, and among them a number of such families settled in Long Island, where they formed the hamlet of Newtown. Unable to support a minister and to maintain a church building of their own, they joined hands with others of the same faith at Flushing, and for a number of years worshipped there, until December 2, 1731, when a meeting of the resident members in Newtown was called to form plans for the establishment of a church organisation of their own and to devise means for the erection of a house of worship upon land contributed by Peter Berrien. At a subsequent meeting held on May 27, a committee was appointed which at once began active operations for the erection of a meeting-house at the intersection of Broadway and Union Avenue in Newtown.

The building they erected conformed to the usual style of the early Dutch churches in this section of the country, being octagonal in shape, with a roof ascending from each side, while a cupola perched upon its apex, and within was the usual narrow and lofty pulpit, with its inevitable sounding-board. One side of the church was used for the seating of the male members of the congregation and the other for the women.

For two years, during the Revolutionary War, the British used the old church for a powder magazine, while the church members held intermittent meetings in the houses of various members of the congregation.

In 1828 the trustees secured its incorporation under the laws of the State of New York, and in 1831 the old meeting-house was torn down to make room for the present church. The corner stone of this later structure, which is built in the Colonial style, was laid on September 16, 1831, and the church was dedicated on July 29, 1832. Into this new structure were brought many of the furnishings that had been used during the ninety-eight years' occupancy of the old meeting-house.

In 1854 one of the members of the congregation erected a chapel adjoining the church building, and ten years later the consistory of the Church organised a mission at Winfield, erecting there in 1880 a substantial and handsome structure.

A sale of land donated to the church by one of its members netted so handsome a sum that in the spring of 1906 the church edifice was thoroughly renovated, even to the extent of a generous enlargement of the structure, though the Colonial style was carefully preserved. The chapel was brought to a level with the church building and a covered passageway constructed to connect the two. On each side of this passageway were built church parlours to encourage social gatherings among the members of the congregation. New windows were placed throughout the church building and a new pulpit and choir platform erected. The main auditorium was completely remodelled, and being arched, groined, and decorated, was made most attractive. The organ was rebuilt and a water motor introduced to operate it.

In the belfry of the Reformed Dutch Church of Newtown swings the bell that has summoned the congregation to worship during the past one hundred and fifteen years. It was cast in Holland in 1792.

From the number of missionary stations founded by the Newtown church and the careful guard she has preserved over their welfare, it has come to be regarded as the mother church throughout Queens County. Among the offspring of this church may be named the churches at Astoria, East Williamsburg, Long Island

City, Steinway, Ridgewood and the Second German Church of Newtown.

The one hundred and seventy-fifth anniversary of the founding of the church organisation took place during the week beginning Sunday, March 10, 1907, and brought together members of widely scattered families whose ancestors had been closely allied with the history of the Church.

THE OLD PALATINE CHURCH

IN THE MOHAWK VALLEY

THE marriage of the eldest daughter of King James II. of England to William of Orange naturally resulted, when William and Mary came to the English throne, in the emigration of many Germans to the British Isles. In these Protestant Germans, Mary's sister, Queen Anne, evidently became deeply interested, for she aided them in every way possible, donating for their support large tracts of land in America and sending out numerous colonies of them at the expense of the royal treasury.

During Queen Anne's reign, in 1706, one such colony sent out to the Mohawk Valley met in each other's homes for worship until on June 2, 1729, they dedicated their first house of God. It was a rude structure built of logs, surrounded by a palisade for protection against the Indians, and lacking flooring and chimney. A roughly-built pulpit and homely seats were all its furniture, but the people rejoiced in it at last as a building of their own, consecrated to the worship of God. Queen Anne sent them a silver communion service, and the glebe about the church was also a gift from her.

The little church passed through many trying vicissitudes, including attacks by hostile Indians, before it was replaced in 1770 by the stone structure which is still standing and occupied regularly for service. This stone church is on the river road in what is now the little town of Palatine, and draws its membership from both sides of the river. Before its erection there had been no resident minister, the congregation being served by a Lutheran minister who came from Stone Arabia, some five or six miles distant.

The edifice, which is known as the "Palatine Stone Church," was dedicated August 18, 1770. In architectural design, with its gambrel roof, it differs from most of the ancient church buildings that have survived to our own day. Originally, the entrance opened toward the north, and over it was inserted a large rectangular stone bearing an inscription in German and the date of dedication. This front door was closed in 1868 and two doors opened at the easterly end of the structure. A gallery runs around three sides of the interior. The pulpit originally stood directly opposite the entrance, in shape resembling a tall goblet, reached by a staircase which wound round the stem. Above it hung the sounding-board, which together with the pulpit was painted drab. The pews had high, straight backs that forbade

sleeping and were painted a " Spanish brown "
in the prevailing style of the day.

The old pews have been remodelled and the
old pulpit has given place to a more modern one,
but the large square pews on each side of it retain
their original form. The old gallery has disappeared, and the old-time bell was long ago replaced by one which for sweetness of tone is
famous throughout the whole Mohawk Valley.

On August 18, 1870, the Church held a centennial service, which brought together many widely-
scattered descendants of its original founders.

CENTER CHURCH

NEW HAVEN, CONNECTICUT

IN 1637 John Davenport and a little band of followers came to Quinnipiac, seeking religious freedom. For months they worshipped under immense oak trees, and finally on April 18, 1838, dedicated a house of worship erected upon the ground they had already hallowed with their prayers. During the previous winter, when the weather had been intensely cold, services had been held regularly in the barn of Robert Newman.

On June 4, 1639, a meeting was called to effect a union between the Separatists and the Puritans. With a spirit of remarkable toleration, each sect regarded the opinions of the other as individual and not forbidding their admittance into so close a relationship as one church body. The final organisation was accomplished and seven elders chosen from the two differing sects to administer the church affairs on August 22. So broad was their platform that to secure membership in the church the candidate was required only to acknowledge his belief in Christianity.

The structure erected by the members of this

Center Church, New Haven, Connecticut

union was used not only for religious services, but also as a general court. The building
was only fifty feet square, and when the erection
of a tower was considered, the framework was
found to be too light to support its weight. The
tower was therefore shored up on posts, and these
in time showing signs of decay, in January,
1660, the congregation convened to determine a
remedy. No more economical measures having
been suggested, both the tower and the turret
were taken down carefully, and the old shoring
replaced with new.

To provide against unexpected Indian attacks
a sentinel stood watch every Sabbath in this
turret, while armed guards patrolled the road in
the vicinity of the meeting-house. The charg-
ing and training of two cannon before service
added to the feeling of security of the worshippers. With that spirit of intense practicality that
marked all their procedures, provision was made
to prevent any women or children ascending to
the turret during divine service, that the attention
of the sentinel might not be distracted from his
duty. A spirit of martial law was also evidenced
by the beating of a drum as a signal to assemble
for worship.

By 1662 the congregation had so increased in
numbers that seats were brought in until the
aisles were too crowded for passage. Low
benches were erected along the side walls to ac-

commodate the younger people of the congregation and later another gallery was added.

In this church the custom arose of standing while the minister read the text for the day.

In 1669 the congregation began seriously to consider the erection of another building for the better accommodation of the attendants, but no contractor could be found willing to erect such a structure as was desired for the amount offered. It was finally decided to enlarge the present edifice, with a result far from artistic. The windows in the new portion were larger than the old ones; the new lumber made the old clapboards look rusty; and even the subsequent boarding over of the old portion of the meeting-house and the enlarging of the original windows did not mend matters. Finally, on November 14, 1770, the meeting-house was sold at auction, and the congregation erected a new structure. Eleven years later, in 1681, they purchased a bell, and from that time the beating of the drum as a call to worship was abandoned. The bell was also rung as a curfew at nine o'clock each evening.

The third church edifice was built in 1757, upon the original site, to be succeeded in 1814 by the present structure, which, with its stately pillars and tall steeple, presents a dignified and beautiful appearance, standing in the centre of the spacious green.

A stained-glass window in the church depicts

a scene commemorative of the preaching of the pioneer, Davenport, under a wide-spreading oak tree; the women and children grouped about him tell the story of the journeying of his flock through the wilderness from Salem to the Connecticut shore, while a seven-branched candlestick symbolises the seven elders who planned the original church organisation.

Center Church is regarded with deep affection by the alumni of Yale University, as the graduating exercises have been held within its walls for a century. In the graveyard about the church lie many of the pioneers of the city; among them three of the judges who voted for the execution of Charles I. find a quiet resting place.

ST. JOHN'S CHURCH

PORTSMOUTH, NEW HAMPSHIRE

THE site on which St. John's Church, in Portsmouth, New Hampshire, was erected, and which came to be known as "Church Hill," was the gift of an Englishman, a resident of the village. In honour of Caroline Wilhelmina of Anspach, wife of King George II. of England, in whose reign the little church sprang up, the parishioners named it "Queen's Chapel," and the Queen sent the parish a prayer book, a silver communion service and a Bible, which latter is now one of the most cherished possessions of the Church as well as intrinsically the most valuable. It was one of four copies of an edition which had been stricken off by the printer before the discovery of the error in the New Testament which substitutes "vinegar" for "vineyard," known to collectors as the "vinegar" Bible.

In 1732 a more substantial structure succeeded the little "Queen's Chapel," and the parish then took to itself the name of the beloved disciple. The first rector of the church, the Reverend Arthur Brown, is known to history as the clergyman who performed the ceremony that made Governor Wentworth and his humble maid-servant, Martha Hilton, man and wife. The old bell that summoned the ancient parish to worship also deserves special mention. It had originally hung in the French Cathedral in Louisburg, Cape Breton, and was one of the prizes secured in the capture of that city on April 4, 1745.

When the American Colonies declared their independence the objectionable prayers for the English sovereign and his family provided in the Book of Common Prayer were obliterated at St. John's by the simple process of pasting over them slips of paper on which were printed prayers for Congress and the success of the patriot army. Money was scarce and prayer books too costly to be cast aside. Years later an English officer, finding one of these old prayer books in the pew he occupied in the little church, cut out the leaf as a relic.

On December 24, 1806, St. John's was burned, and the supports of the belfry giving way, let the bell sink to the ground with such force as to crack it seriously. The parish sent it to Boston to be recast by no less notable a person than Paul Revere, and at the same time set about the erection of a new house of worship, in which they hung the bell in place again, where it still rings the New England curfew.

One of the most notable ministrations of St.

John's Church is the " Church dole," instituted by Colonel Thomas Atkinson, who daily brought in person for the needy of the parish a liberal supply of bread and placed it in the baptismal font where all the poor in the town could freely partake of it.   The members of the parish still observe this custom.

The church organ was first imported by a Boston congregation in 1713, and after various vicissitudes came into the possession of St. John's in 1836.   Among the relics preserved by the Church is a credence table made from wood that was once a part of the United States Frigate *Hartford,* Admiral Farragut's flagship when he captured New Orleans.   The church equipment, indeed, has been gathered from all parts of the world, the baptismal font being a trophy taken by Captain Thomas Mason from the French at the capture of Senegal on the west coast of Africa.

TRINITY CHURCH

NEW YORK CITY

THE " English Church," as the Protestant
Episcopal Church was called in the New
Netherlands, largely superseded the
Dutch Reformed Church when the English con-
querors took possession of Manhattan.   The
little chapel within the fort was named " King's
Chapel " and the liturgy was read in it until
1697, when Trinity Church was completed.

The first, and original, Trinity Church was
nearly a year in building, though it was but a
small, square structure.   It stood on the west
side of Broadway, and a slope of green lawn
behind it ran down to the Hudson River.   In
1737 an enlargement of the church building was
undertaken, and completed in 1739, increasing
its dimensions to one hundred and forty-eight
feet in length by seventy in width.   At the same
time a steeple one hundred and seventy feet in
height was added.

The church occupied this edifice until 1776,
when it was destroyed by a fire which threatened
the whole town four days after the British Gen-

eral Howe had seized the city. Little effort was
made to rebuild until after the close of the Revolution, when, in 1788, a new building rose over
the old ruins. It fell far short of the ample
dimensions of its predecessor, but served the
needs of the parish until about 1841, when they
laid the corner stone of a third church, the present "Trinity," which was consecrated in May,
1846.

From this "mother in Israel" went forth various offspring as the family became too numerous
and widely scattered to meet in the old church.
Under her faithful wing three other charges—
St. George's, St. Paul's and St. John's Chapels,
grew up, the first becoming an independent parish in 1849, while St. Paul's and St. John's are
still chapels of Old Trinity.

At the outset of its career Trinity Church
owned a large tract of land to which was added
a magnificent endowment from the English
Government—the gift of "Queen's Farm," embodying all that tract of land lying between
Vesey Street on the south and Christopher
Street on the north, and running from Broadway to the Hudson River. A greater part of
this domain is still in the possession of the
church, which derives a large income from it.
From this source comes the sustenance of the
parish church, as well as some six chapels, while
upon the bounty of the mother church depend

Trinity Church, New York City

numerous charitable organisations as well as
many indigent churches in various sections of
the city.

The charities of Old Trinity and its chapels
are numerous and liberal. The Employment Society connected with the parish furnishes sewing
for destitute women, while the Sisterhood of the
Holy Cross provides for the care of the poor
and sick, and Trinity Chapel House gives shelter and sustenance to the aged communicants of
the Chapel. Parochial and mission schools are
maintained, as well as an infirmary for the sick
of the parish. A Working Club brings together
working men, providing them club rooms and a
watchful care, and at the last a decent burial.

Trinity Association is composed of gentlemen
active in the charitable work of the parish. It
supports the Mission Home, including a young
men's guild, a boys' guild, a summer seashore
sanitarium, and a relief bureau, and it dispenses
entertainment for the needy, as well as maintaining a school to train young girls in house-
work.

In the churchyard around Old Trinity lie
many who have been conspicuous in the his-
tory of our country. Here rest Alexander
Hamilton, Judge Watts, and Robert Fulton.
One monument recalls to the passersby on
Broadway the story of those who died in the
British prison ships, and whose remains still re-

pose within the shadow of the first Church of England in New York City. Here, too, we find the last resting place of Captain James Lawrence who lost his life defending his battleship, *Chesapeake,* against the British frigate *Shannon* in the war of 1812. The oldest tombstone in the churchyard is dated 1681. It is that of a child, Richard Churcher, who died at the age of five years and five months, and whose sandstone slab, with skull, cross bones and winged hourglass, has endured to this day.

ST. PAUL'S

The most interesting of the Trinity chapels is St. Paul's, at Broadway and Vessey Street. Standing now with its back to Broadway, the present building was begun in 1756, and is the oldest church edifice in the city of New York. In the graveyard are monuments to the Irish patriot Emmet, G. F. Cooke, the actor; and a memorial to General Montgomery, who fell at Quebec, and whose body was brought to New York for a second interment. Authorised by Congress this monument was bought in France by Benjamin Franklin and brought over in an American privateer that was captured by a British gunboat before it could land the memorial safely. The old organ of St. Paul's, which was played on the day of Washington's inauguration, was afterwards sold to St. Michael's in Marblehead, Massachusetts.

Among the square pews of St. Paul's are those occupied by Washington and General Clinton, indicated by tablets set in the adjacent walls. During the days of the English occupation Lord Howe, Major André, and Sir Guy Carleton are also said to have worshipped here. Washington indeed attended service in St. Paul's the day of his inauguration.

ST. JOHN'S

St. John's Chapel in Varick Street, another chapel of Trinity, built in 1807, is still picturesquely standing. At one time its neighbourhood was one of the most fashionable in the city, having a park, St. John's Park, the use of which was restricted to neighbouring householders, as Gramercy Park is to-day.

ST. MARK'S

St. Mark's Church, at Tenth Street and Second Avenue, occupies the site of an older Dutch church, an interesting relic of which is preserved in a memorial stone to old Peter Stuyvesant, captain-general and governor in chief of New Amsterdam, who died in 1675. A great grandson, also named Peter Stuyvesant, and a

Trinity vestryman, gave the site and surrounding lots to St. Mark's, whose cornerstone was laid in 1795. It was in this churchyard that the remains of A. T. Stewart were laid to rest, and from which they were afterward mysteriously stolen.

CHRIST CHURCH

BENNINGTON, VERMONT

THE first church building erected by the parish of Christ Church at Bennington, Vermont, was dedicated on February 11, 1762. The funds that could be raised for its construction were not large and the little edifice was simple in style, being but two stories in height and utterly devoid of a steeple. The pews were of the variety then in vogue, square and high-backed, though the railings along their tops were unusually ornamental.

This church building not only served the inhabitants of Bennington for a "town-hall" where all gatherings of any importance were held, but its upper story also did duty as a school. Many notable meetings have taken place within its walls. Among the most memorable of these was a service of public thanksgiving when the news reached Bennington of the capture of Ticonderoga by the "Green Mountain Boys," an occasion of such importance that Ethan Allen made a hurried visit to his home in Bennington in order to be present, bringing with him a host of prisoners of war.

In Christ Church the State legislature first met, and later, in default of a courthouse, it was the scene of one of the most noted murder trials in the early days of Vermont. At an early period, too, the little parish was torn by the great American question of slavery, in 1778 dissensions arising among the members over this national difficulty. The cause of the freedman won, when, on November 18, 1779, a negro woman who had been taken captive on Lake . Champlain with a number of British officers and troops, publicly received her freedom in the little Episcopal house of worship. The opposition to slavery grew more and more intense, while the minority in favour of it became more decided in the parish, until disruption would have threatened the Church had not the rector and the more peace-loving members averted such a disaster.

With the exception of this one difference of opinion, nothing has marred the harmony that has existed in the parish since its organisation. The little church, remodelled and fitted up in more modern style since the early days, is still occupied for divine worship.

THE OLD SHIP CHURCH

HINGHAM, MASSACHUSETTS

IN the old town of Hingham, Massachusetts, stands one of the quaint religious landmarks of New England—the Old Ship meeting-house, which dates from the year 1680. So skilfully was its framework put together and so carefully were the timbers selected that it seems destined to survive still longer as a memorial to the piety of its early builders.

The land whereon the Old Ship Church was built was purchased from one Captain Hobart, and within six months from the time the building was begun it was ready for occupancy, being dedicated to divine worship in January, 1682. Its style of architecture exemplifies the severe taste of the New England colonists; it is rectangular in shape and two stories in height, with a truncated pyramidal roof surmounted by a belfry, which in addition to holding the bell also served as a lookout station. The peculiar appearance of the church is responsible for the title by which it has so long been known—the Old Ship. Surmounting the belfry is a weather-vane, while from the bell a rope dangles down

in the centre aisle to the floor of the church. A
two-storied porch projects from the middle of
the south side. The only material change made
in the exterior during the two and one-quarter
centuries since it was erected is the small porch
added to the west side.

The interior of the church is as bare and pro-
saic as those of other early churches in New
England, all ideas of elaboration seeming to
exhaust themselves upon the belfry. The outer
walls of the church were devoid of paint, while
the interior lacked the luxury of any heating
apparatus. The congregation worshipped under
bare rafters, and sat on the plainest of wooden
benches, hewn out by hand and without backs.
During the many years that have intervened
since the Reverend Peter Hobart preached
against the sin of hoop-skirts and the congregation gathered to discuss means of preventing
Indian depredations, there has been virtually no
change in the interior of this house of worship
except for the addition of the stoves which superseded the old foot-warmers, and of the more
comfortable seats that were put in about 1817.

Prominent in the front of the church stood
a pew for the elders and another for the deacons, while a third was set aside for the accommodation of the widow of the first pastor. The
pulpit, reached by a stairway on one side, is a
massive structure which is, nevertheless, over-

The Old Ship Church, Hingham, Massachusetts

shadowed by a curiously contrived canopy answering for a sounding-board. The surroundings of the church are quite in harmony with the building itself, being entirely of an older world than the modern railway station in full sight of the ancient edifice.

In 1763 a meeting of the congregation took place to consider the assigning of seats to " persons skilled in musick," and in 1802 a bass viol was purchased to aid in the service. Additions of a violin, a flute, a bassoon and a clarinet followed, gradually paving the way for the introduction of an organ in 1866.

In point of usefulness as well as antiquity no church edifice in our country has a more enviable record. Bishop Meade in his eulogy of the church says that there exists nowhere within the original limits of the United States a house for public worship as old as the meeting-house of the First Parish in Hingham which still continues to be used for the purpose for which it was originally erected and still remains on the site where it was built. Like many another early New England meeting-house, the Old Ship has also done other service than merely providing a place for worship. For more than one hundred years it was used for all town meetings and village gatherings.

CAROLINE CHURCH

SETAUKET, LONG ISLAND

THE organisation of the first parish of the Protestant Episcopal Church on Long Island was accomplished at Setauket in 1725, and in five years the communicants were financially able to erect a house of worship. With the exception of this little church at Setauket none of the original Episcopalian Church structures on Long Island are standing at the present day.

Founded in a settlement in which staunch Puritans greatly outnumbered them, the members of the little parish were bound the more closely together by the persecution of their neighbours. The town meeting went so far as to enjoin the rector from the use of the Book of Common Prayer at any public meeting lest he distress "some tender conscience," and things steadily tended from bad to worse.

At a meeting of the Episcopalian clergy held in New York City October 5, 1704, the rector of Trinity called attention to the fact that while missionaries were being sent abroad to convert the heathen, yet almost at the doors of New York—at the eastern end of Long Island—a handful of churchmen and women planted in the midst of Puritans were without comfort and provision for their spiritual guidance. From that time the needs of the Long Island churchmen received greater attention, and missionaries visited them at stated intervals. The Reverend John Sharpe, the chaplain of the military forces of New York, included Setauket regularly in his tours of inspection and invariably held service there.

Upon its erection in 1730 the little church at Setauket had originally been named "Christ Church," but when Queen Caroline, the wife of George II., sent over a communion service of silver, and linen for the altar, the style in recognition of this gracious act was changed to "The Caroline Protestant Episcopal Church."

In spite of a lack of funds that forbade the supporting of a resident rector, and of continued opposition to all ritualistic forms of worship, the little parish prospered, and by 1844 numbered some two hundred communicants. Many a missionary spirit went forth from it, and parishes here and there along the whole of the southern coast of Long Island regard it as their parent church. A number of its parish rectors have been called to other positions of high trust, and when its centennial services were held in 1830, its sons and daughters, with their children and grandchildren, gathered in great numbers to show their reverence for the " Mother Church of Long Island."

THE ROMAN CATHOLIC CATHEDRAL

THE CITY OF MEXICO

BY far the most gorgeous church building in North America is the Roman Catholic Cathedral (Church of the Asuncion de María Santissima) in the City of Mexico, which is moreover, in point of area covered, one of the largest churches in the world.

The Cathedral was built according to instructions from Philip II. of Spain, and the process of erection consumed almost a century, from 1573 to 1667. The cost of construction is estimated to have been two million dollars, though most of the actual labour was performed by slaves. The form of the building is that of a cross, and it is four hundred and twenty-eight feet long, two hundred feet wide, and one hundred and seventy-six feet high at the dome, while its massive twin towers rise to a height of more than two hundred feet.

The ground occupied by the Cathedral is historical, being the site of the great pyramidal teocalli, or temple of the Aztec god Huitzilo-

pachtli. The principal façade has three en-
trances and is flanked by two tall towers. At
the base of one of these stands the celebrated
Aztec calendar, an enormous granite monolith
which was brought there at the expense of infinite labour in 1790.

The interior is very rich, and the building is
a treasure house of art, since for centuries the
Roman Catholic Church in Mexico was rich
enough to command the best art products in
the world. The Cathedral is a superb memorial
of the time, indeed, when the Catholic Church
possessed two-thirds of the entire wealth of
Mexico.

The Altar of the Kings, in the apse, which attracts the attention of the visitor immediately, is
made wholly of highly wrought and polished
silver, and is covered with a profusion of crosses
and ornaments of pure gold. In the nearby
aisles are buried many whose names are closely
associated with the history of the Mexican nation. To this same altar in 1811 were brought
for burial the heads of Hidalgo, Allende, Al-
dema and Jimines from the prison of Guanjusro,
after they had been condemned to death and
executed, after having been excommunicated by
the Church as heretics and traitors. Before this
altar, also, on May 22, 1822, Augustin de Itur-
bide was crowned the first emperor of Mexico,
with the title of Augustin I., and two years later,

The Roman Catholic Cathedral, City of Mexico

after his execution, his body was brought to lie
beneath it.   Forty years afterward took place
the coronation of the ill-fated Maximilian.   In
1857 the triumphant government of Juarez
seized the golden candlesticks and the gold and
jewelled statue of the Assumption, to procure
through their sale funds for the new Republican
party.   This statue, bedecked as it was with
diamonds, has been estimated to have been worth
over a million dollars.

Along each side of the central altar runs a
balustrade, enclosing a space some eight feet in
width and from eighty to one hundred feet
in length.   This balustrade is four or five feet in
height and the top rail from six to eight inches
in thickness.   On the top of this hand-rail and
about six or eight feet apart are human images,
most beautifully wrought and about two feet
in height.   These are utilised as candelabra.   The
balustrade, the hand-rail and the images are
made from an amalgam of gold, silver and copper.   An estimate can be made of their value
from the fact that some years ago an offer was
made to purchase it complete, replace it with one
of solid silver, and pay an additional million dollars into the bargain.   Here and there about the
Cathedral are other similar hand-rails and balustrades, in smaller proportions—in all some four
hundred feet—made from this same amalgam.
These balustrades encircle six altars in various

portions of the building, there being no less than fourteen chapels altogether.

In the chapter house near by is a Madonna and Child said to be a genuine Murillo. Other fine paintings hang here and there in the Cathedral.

The church bell—the Santa María Guadalupe —is nineteen feet long, and with the exception of the great bell in Moscow is the largest in the world.

Throughout the edifice appear vases, paintings, images and ornaments of silver, gold, and precious stones; in some portions seeming to reach from floor to ceiling. Though the Catholic Church does not invite investigation into its wealth, even the precious metals and jewels that are found displayed in the Cathedral of Mexico strike the beholder with wonder. And when one takes into consideration the treasure that lies hidden away from sight in the vast vaults of the Cathedral, he gains an idea of the immense wealth that has been lavished upon the church. Instinctively the mind recalls Montezuma and the riches that were brought forward to purchase his ransom.

THE PRESBYTERIAN CHURCH

SOUTHAMPTON, LONG ISLAND

EARLY in the spring of the year 1640 a little band of staunch Presbyterians set out from Lynn, Massachusetts, to seek a home where they might worship God in accordance with the dictates of their own consciences. They sailed along the coast of Long Island and made their first landing on May 10 at its west end. This, however, brought them into too close contact with the Dutch in Manhattan and led to unpleasant relations. Re-embarking, the little company sailed eastward again and on the 12th of the next month made the first permanent settlement on the east coast of Long Island, giving it the name of " Southampton."

They were joined presently by others from their old home in Lynn, for in November, 1640, the Reverend Abraham Pierson was ordained a minister of the gospel in Lynn and together with seven or eight Presbyterian families from that section set sail also for Southampton. As the months went on many others were added to their number. Some who came from Europe, after a brief stay in Lynn, went on to Long Island and became identified there with those of their own faith, so that the Southampton settlement flourished, and the membership of the little church increased rapidly.

In its form of church government the settlement was independent, the name Presbyterian not being associated with the organisation until seventy years later, when the town donated land for the erection of a new house of worship. This deed was made to the "Presbyterian Church." That the titles of "Deacon" and "Elder" were in use previous to this date is evidenced by a number of gravestones in the little churchyard. In September, 1716, the church requested the Presbytery of Philadelphia to send to them, as minister, the Reverend Samuel Gelston, promising thereafter to "subject themselves to the Presbytery in the Lord." The first meeting of the Presbytery of Long Island was held in the Southampton Church April 17, 1717. The isolation of the church resulted in its being left without representation in many later meetings of the Synod, but the members have regarded themselves as members of the Presbyterian Church ever since their call to the Philadelphia Presbytery in 1716.

Soon after the formation of the colony, in 1640, a log church building was erected, a simple and inexpensive structure, representing the labour of the members' own hands. Ten years afterward the building was leased to one Thomas Goldsmith with the provision that he maintain it for three years as " an ordinary for strangers," and in March, 1651, the erection of a new house of worship was undertaken, the new building measuring twenty-four by twenty feet. It was ready for occupancy in 1653 and served the congregation until 1707, when a third structure was put up. In the interim between the disposal of the first house of worship and the completion of the second, religious services took place regularly in the house of one of the elders of the church.

The church erected in 1707 continued to serve as a house of worship for the congregation until 1844. In 1821 it was thoroughly remodelled, but, being found too small some twenty years later to accommodate the congregation, was sold to a little band of Methodists whose church organisation had just been effected, the Presbyterian Church then erecting for themselves the edifice that is now in use.

THE FIRST CONGREGATIONAL CHURCH

DOVER, NEW HAMPSHIRE

THE early colonists who settled in and about Dover, New Hampshire, cannot be said to have fled from any persecution. A more material cause occasioned their removal to this locality—the better opportunity to ply their trade of fishermen. Yet though they were a simple folk, rude and uncultured when they came to Dover in 1638, they brought with them their chosen minister of the Gospel, and during the following year erected a rude church, built of logs roughly hewn. The walls were provided for protection against the weather with a coat of plaster both inside and out. The minister who came with the colonists declined to stay after the first year, since the living was precarious and he was unable to reconcile himself to the action of the members of the Dover congregation in excluding all whose creed did not harmonise with their own.

These Dover colonists were particularly bent on having their own way in worship. The ear-

The First Congregational Church, Dover, New Hampshire

lier settlers combated most vigorously an attempt made by Quakers to secure land for a settlement in their immediate vicinity, so much so that after being roughly handled, the Quakers decided to look for some other spot in which to pitch their tents. The intolerance of the Dover fishermen was a matter of conscience, however, and not of worldly policy; for they sincerely believed toleration of other creeds and other ways of living than their own was sinful. As time went on they became more instead of less intolerant, and religious annals unite in the statement that the Dover Congregational Church was one of the very last to uphold the right of the Church to baptise none but the children of its communicants. It was only at a late day, and under considerable pressure, that the church adopted the "Half-Way Covenant."

On June 28, 1689, in the French and Indian War, came the great massacre that involved all of New England as well as the greater part of New York in its atrocities. Of the membership of the Dover Church, no less than fifty were killed or carried away into captivity. In view of the constant dread that lurked in the minds of these simple people, it is not a matter of surprise that the beating of a drum was their signal to meet for worship at the little church. The ringing of a bell would have served to notify the savages of the absence of many households at church and of the consequent opportunity for pillage.

Sturdy in physique, these Dover fishermen obtained a livelihood where many another people would have starved. They lived in a homely fashion and though their talk was rough and their bearing toward each other and to the world austere, at heart they were honest, God-fearing men.

The noted ecclesiastical quarrel between Knolly and Lakham took place in the little church at Dover. The Puritan, Knolly, marched into the meeting-house armed with his musket in one hand and his Bible in the other. The manner in which he carried his Bible, "mounted on a halbert as an ensign," was meant to show that he depended upon his understanding of the Word of God as one of the most powerful weapons with which to overcome his opponent. The governor came up by boat to Dover, to act as mediator, and finally, after considerable argument, prevailed upon the two adversaries to permit him to appoint a commission of three men, in whom they both had confidence, to settle the matter. This committee deciding that both Knolly and Lakham were in the wrong, naturally each contestant felt himself aggrieved by their judgment.

For that matter every citizen at that time resented outside interference with his church and political rights. When a tree was found marked with an arrow-head—a token of ownership claimed by some absentee—the tree was promptly cut down, since the ownership of the tree would involve the ownership of the land upon which it grew.

The little Dover meeting-house was witness of still another notable incident in the history of the Colony. Once when a sheriff came up to Dover from Massachusetts to collect taxes for the maintenance of the Massachusetts Colony, which claimed New Hampshire as its outlying territory, the residents of Dover resisted the levy as an instance of taxation without representation, and the entire population turned out to the little meeting-house to confront the minion of the law. Upon the sheriff's attempt to arrest the ringleaders in the opposition to the government a serious riot followed, and one liberty-loving woman hurled the pulpit Bible at the sheriff so hard that she knocked him down. So roughly did the people of Dover generally handle him and his assistants that in making his report on the circumstances, he said, "We were glad to escape with our lives."

In the early days fortifications made of logs raised upon earthworks surrounded the meeting-house in the form of a square, portions of which embankment are still traceable. At each corner stood a circular tower, upon which during the hours of worship sentinels were mounted. Out of this enclosure the settlers made many a sortie to drive off Indians that had surrounded the meeting-house.

In 1655 the parish built a new meeting-house on the site of the old. The description of this house of worship is meagre, but that it was of ample dimensions is evidenced by the fact that it is said to have had six windows and twelve doors. Its walls were of plank and the roof of tile. Unlike its predecessor, this building was floored. In 1758 still another structure succeeded it, which in its turn was later altered into a dwelling and sold.

The present church dates from 1829, and its congregation are noted to-day for their intense love of spiritual and political liberty.

SAN XAVIER del BAC

TUCSON, ARIZONA

THE brave missionary work of the Spanish priests in America may be traced in numerous chapels throughout New Mexico and Arizona, most of which are now only ruins. Near Tucson is one of the oldest of these quaint mission churches—that of San Xavier del Bac. So quaint is it in design and so beautiful in architectural execution that one first beholding it can scarcely help an exclamation of surprise and pleasure. Nowhere in the Southwest is there anything that approaches it in beauty of form and colour, or melancholy charm.

Time has dealt ruthlessly with the green wooden balconies in its front and has broken out their floors, but the original sweet-toned bronze bells still hang in one of the towers, and the pediment of the façade is ornamented with escutcheons, lions rampant, and wreaths of foliage. Niches here and there still hold dilapidated bizarre statues, and ornate pilasters flank the main entrance—the whole moulded in stucco upon a foundation of brick. Spots from which the plaster has fallen away disclose the fact that the pilasters are held together by a centering rod of timber.

The designer, whoever he may have been, was evidently inspired by Venetian-Byzantine traditions. The church is roofed with numerous simple domes and half domes. The interiors of these are frescoed with angels and evangelists, and the chancel walls almost covered with gilding, now stained and battered, while the painted and gilded lions on the chancel rails inevitably recall St. Mark's in Venice.

Though the inscription of the date of the building of the church is partially obscured, with care it is discernible in the façade—1768. The present edifice is situated upon the site occupied by the original mission chapel built about 1654. Attached to the main chancel piers are large angels, with bannerets, whose draperies are formed of gummed muslin or a preparation similar to papier-maché, while a painted and gilded Virgin looks down from a high altar niche. The whole interior has an air of mediæval richness and obscurity most unusual in the Western hemisphere. Since the foundation of the church toward the end of the seventeenth century it is said that its services have never been discontinued.

THE DUTCH REFORMED CHURCH

HERKIMER, NEW YORK

AMONG the quaintest and most curious of antiquities in New York State are the ancient stone churches erected through the mediation of Queen Anne on the banks of the Mohawk River. Their number is now reduced to three—Queen Anne's Chapel at Fort Hunter and the Dutch churches of Caughnawaga and Fort Herkimer. Of these the church at Fort Herkimer is the only one still used for divine worship.

It is evident from its heavy masonry that this church was intended to last for ages, for not only are its walls three feet thick, but the corners of the building are buttressed and the roof runs to a solid, lofty peak like a pyramid. This extra strength was to serve as protection against attacks by Indians, as in many another early church. Unlike many other churches known, this one exercised foresight in its building, and that it might provide ample room for later settlers, was made much larger than was actually required by the number of communicants reckoned in its fold.

Within, a broad gallery, huge and clumsy in construction, extends along three sides, and ungainly columns of untutored carpentry support the lofty roof. The pews are square, with straight backs. The pulpit is one of the greatest curiosities to be found in ecclesiastical architecture in America. Shaped in the form of a drum, it is perched on a pedestal at what at first seems almost a fearful height, and is reached by a steep and winding staircase. Having safely accomplished the ascent of these narrow, winding stairs, the minister literally looked down upon his flock, who sat with necks bent back in their endeavour to see and hear him. A gaudy red cushion, upon which rested the Bible, decorated the pulpit, while on a bracket near by and in full view of both minister and congregation, stood the hourglass. Above the pulpit, like an extinguisher, hung the ancient sounding board.

For over one hundred years after its erection the church was without flooring or means of heating. It was the scene of many an Indian attack in both the Indian wars and the Revolution. During the Revolution, however, Sir William Johnson, and later his protégé, Joseph Brant, assumed the protection of the church, and it escaped serious injury, while its stout walls made an excellent refuge for the settlers of the neighbourhood.

The Dutch Reformed Church, Fort Herkimer, New York

After the close of the war the parishioners added a second story and thoroughly repaired the interior. The woodwork about the pulpit was decorated with mouldings painted like a checkerboard in red and white. With rare good judgment those who had charge of the restoration of the church refrained from altering the antique pulpit or the communion table, both of quaint and old time pattern—the handiwork, no doubt, of some honest German artisan in Frankfort or Heidelberg.

From this ancient tabernacle many an offshoot has sprung, and for many miles around Herkimer may be found church organisations which trace their origin back to the mother church at " German Flatts." To-day the communicants still occupy the church building regularly each Sunday, and regard it with a feeling of most intense reverence.

THE FIRST CHURCH OF CHRIST

SAYBROOK, CONNECTICUT

IN 1646 there was organised in the "Great Hall" of Saybrook, Connecticut, a body that was destined to exercise throughout the whole State a powerful influence in both ecclesiastical and political circles. This organisation, which was termed the "First Church of Christ," in the ensuing year began the erection of a suitable house of worship. The site chosen was at the end of the public square or "Green." Of the plan of this building no description remains, nor of the materials that entered into its construction, though the protection it provided against sudden attacks by Indians is most definitely recorded.

A second church succeeded the first meeting-house in 1681, built on the same site. This second structure was plain in design, as was usual in the early days of New England. Its seats were plain wooden benches, without backs, and were assigned to members of the congregation "according to rank, age, office and estate." Several leading men received permission to build for their families, at their own expense, square pews to the right of the pulpit. The pulpit itself, high and of angular construction, was reached by a winding stair, and furnished with a Geneva Bible, a Bay Psalm Book, and an hourglass by which the service could be strictly timed. During service two deacons invariably faced the congregation, occupying seats at the base of the pulpit, while the tithing-man with his fox-tail rod was stationed where he could best observe the behaviour of the congregation.

This building in 1726 was replaced by a third church at a cost of sixteen hundred dollars. By the end of the century a bell and a steeple were added, and the bell was rung regularly at noontime, announcing to the residents of Saybrook that the hour for dinner had arrived, until 1840. Neither of the first two church buildings was provided with stoves or any other means of keeping warm—a condition which continued in the third church building for one hundred years after it was erected.

One of the chief features of the third church was the exceptionally high pulpit, overhung with a huge sounding-board, both being ornamented with panels and elaborate mouldings. Each Sunday the stairs leading to the pulpit were occupied by small boys, among whom great rivalry existed regarding the occupancy of the upper step, since the lad so seated had the privilege of opening the pulpit door for the minister.

The pews were square in form and ample in accommodation. Seats were provided on three sides, hung on rude hinges which permitted them to be raised parallel with the backs, like choir-stalls, and afford more standing room. Around three sides of the building ran a wide gallery, heavily and most substantially built, the east wing of which was assigned to women and the west to men. The front tier of seats was reserved for the " singers," while behind this were four box pews, considered the most desirable of any in the church. In the extreme rear corner of the gallery stood another box pew, reserved for the use of coloured people, who were not permitted to sit in any other portion of the church.

In the second structure occupied by the First Church of Christ in Saybrook there met in May, 1708, a convention called by the Great Court of Connecticut, during the session of which the noted " Saybrook Platform " was drawn up. This document, embodying the Articles of Faith, the Discipline and the Authority of the forty churches of Connecticut, was approved by the Court and constituted the ecclesiastical law of the land, Congregationalism becoming the state religion.

Christ Church, West Haven, Connecticut

CHRIST CHURCH

WEST HAVEN, CONNECTICUT

IN the autumn of the year 1722 Connecticut
and indeed all New England was startled
by the announcement that a number of the
brightest and most promising students of Yale
College had declared for Episcopacy. President Woolsey is quoted as saying that greater
alarm could scarcely have been awakened if the
theological faculty had proclaimed themselves
for the Church of Rome, avowing their belief
in transubstantiation and instituting prayers to
the Virgin Mary.

This event alarmed Congregationalism
throughout New England, filling its followers
with great apprehension. The Governor of the
State threw himself into the breach, to aid in
winning back these young men from their de-
fection, but Samuel Johnson, who had already
been ordained to the ministry in the Congregational Church, and his associate tutor in Yale
College, Daniel Browne, stood firm in their
change of faith. Late in the fall of this same
year they sailed together for England and were
regularly ordained in March, 1723, in old St.

Martin's-in-the-Fields, in London. Two weeks afterward, so fate would have it, Daniel Browne died of smallpox and was buried in the church of St. Dunstan's-in-the-West, his only regret being that it had been denied to him to serve in his new faith the people of his native village of West Haven.

Johnson, returning to New England, found, however, a number of staunch churchmen in the neighbourhood of West Haven who greeted him most cordially, recognising at what a sacrifice he had remained faithful to his convictions. They and their families gathered round him, though they were too poor to erect a church building, and had to meet for services wherever accommodations could be found.

The organisation of the parish, such as it was, dates from the return of the Reverend Samuel Johnson from England in 1723. So scattered were the parishioners that they before long divided into two parts, one at Stratford, under the Reverend Mr. Johnson, and the other the West Haven community under the Reverend Jonathan Arnold, who had served for several years as pastor of the Congregational Church in West Haven before he declared for the Church of England. He was no doubt influenced in this decision by the Reverend Samuel Johnson on his occasional visits to West Haven. At all events, he visited Stratford on Easter

Day, 1724, was dismissed from charge of the Congregational Church at West Haven in May or June of that year, and sailed soon after to England to take orders, returning to Connecticut two years later with the appointment of itinerant missionary in that State, with a residence at West Haven.

At this time church and state were scarcely yet divorced, and the new parishes were not without complications. In 1728 the Reverend Mr. Johnson announced that churchmen fortunate enough to reside near the parish churches were exempt from paying tithes to the Congregational ministers, but those scattered through the country districts were still under the necessity of contributing to the church they had abandoned.

The Reverend Samuel Johnson kept a watchful eye over the students of Yale, an alma mater that has supplied many able men to the Episcopal ministry—from Pierson, Palmer and Browne to our own day. So deep, however, lay the prejudice against Episcopacy in New Haven that he was unable to purchase a foot of land on which to erect a chapel. It was only on account of the respect in which he was held and the influence that he gradually gained over many of the students that in time several graduates and a number of young ministers were prevailed upon to read under him. Among these was young Isaac Browne, the brother of Daniel Browne,

who became an under-teacher with Mr. Johnson
at Setauket on Long Island, and who later, having been admitted to orders in England, ministered to the people in New Jersey for many
years.

Although the Reverend Mr. Johnson was able
to conduct service in West Haven but once each
month, he kept in close touch with his people
there and finally secured their ecclesiastical union
with New Haven. With a residence at the former place the Reverend Jonathan Arnold gradually formed outlying parishes in various
sections of Connecticut, extending his labours as
far as Waterbury and Derby, laying in a number
of these localities the foundations of larger parishes than the little mother parish at West Haven
had been able to boast of. He was succeeded in
the home parish in 1740 by the Reverend The-
ophilus Morris, an Englishman, under whose
ministry the first little parish church was erected
in West Haven. The original subscription list
is still extant, very remarkable for the miscel-
laneous articles contributed by those who, with
St. Peter, might have said, "Silver and gold
have I none, but such as I have, give I unto thee."
One finds recorded in it such items as rum, mo-
lasses and mutton, from the proceeds of the sale
of which, nevertheless, the additions to the
church treasury resulted. To raise funds for
even this small structure must have taxed the

resources of these people exceedingly, and the spirit of self-sacrifice of which it is a monument is almost inconceivable at the present day. The original building still stands, though a tower, a chancel and greater breadth on the west side of the body of the church have been added.

In 1742 came that great wave of religious excitement under Whitefield that the Puritans termed the " Great Awakening." The whole country was filled with evangelists, and the fervour reached an extravagance almost beyond belief in many quarters. The old conservative element attempted vainly to stem the tide, showing even greater dislike to the " new lights " than they had shown to Episcopacy. The Episcopal Church itself became a refuge for many who were wearied with the agitation that pervaded every stratum of society and perplexed with such religious turmoil and controversy. It proved a sure foundation—a place where the Gospel alone was preached and the Christian life nourished.

Its history during the past century has been that of many another mother church—her children growing to such a ripe maturity that they no longer needed the supporting arm of their progenitor and became independent parishes. Old families died out and newcomers worshipped according to other forms, the little parish reached evil days, and service was held irregularly, and for a time even was wholly abandoned, and the church building fell into more or less decay. To the Reverend Stephen Jewett of Westville was due the credit of resuming service in the little church on Whit Sunday, 1837. Through his influence the Reverend A. B. Chapin accepted the rectorship two years later, serving the parish most acceptably for ten years. It was during his incumbency that the church was restored in 1841 at a cost of some nine hundred dollars, "making it one of the neatest wood churches in the diocese."

The following year, Bishop Brownell, in his annual address, called the attention of the parishioners to the fact that although the church had stood as a house of worship for one hundred and three years, it had never been consecrated. This ceremony took place accordingly at last on May 19, 1842, in the presence not only of the communicants then living in the vicinity of the church, but also of hundreds of the descendants of the pioneer members of the parish, who came from every section of New England to participate in the service.

TRINITY CHURCH

FISHKILL, NEW YORK

WHENEVER and wherever Church of England communicants entered into the settlements of the Puritans, they were made to feel most keenly that they were "without the fold." Not only did the Puritans refuse the use of such church buildings as were already erected, but in many instances forbade the holding of any pulpit service in which the Book of Common Prayer should be used. This attitude of hostility was especially manifest against the communicants of Trinity Church, organised in Fishkill, New York, in 1756, under the able leadership of the Right Reverend Samuel Seabury—America's first Protestant Episcopal Bishop. They persisted in their faith nevertheless, and that same year secured their first rector, the Reverend John Beardsley, whose simplicity of character, gentleness, and tact won for the little church the good will and regard even of its opponents.

The present church edifice was erected in September, 1769. It was a comely structure, with a tall, tapering spire, surmounted by a ball and weather vane, in the customary style of the churches of that period. The earlier records of the parish were lost during the Revolution, but it is a matter of history that the church was used by General Washington as a military hospital at the time the Continental Army disbanded in 1783. Still further historic interest arises from the fact that on September 3, 1776, the New York Provincial Convention removed to Trinity Church from White Plains, where Washington then had his headquarters.

On December 16, 1777, the rector of the parish, the Reverend John Beardsley, was summoned to New York City by the Council of Safety, and for nine years the little flock was without any shepherd save such as might occasionally visit that section of the State.

After the close of the war the Reverend Henry Van Duke undertook the reorganisation of the parish, and his energy and ability resulted in the healing of various breaches between opposing political factions, as well as the restoration of the church building, and a considerable increase in the number of communicants.

On November 21, 1789, Trinity Church witnessed the signing in a State Convention of the ratification of the Constitution of the United States by the State of New York, an act accomplished in the presence of many interested communicants.

In 1803 subscriptions were solicited through-out the parish to raise money for the purpose of strengthening the church steeple, which, however, seems still to have continued a source of anxiety on account of its weakness, and in 1817 was re-moved. The base remained, and until 1860 supported a short tower surmounted by an or-namental railing. In 1860 this tower was razed and the whole building thoroughly repaired. A few years later the parish remodelled the interior of the church, removing the high pulpit, with its antiquated sounding-board, which had stood near the centre of the building, and replacing the high-backed pews with more comfortable seats.

In the churchyard of Trinity lie many of the most prominent of the earlier colonists in or near Fishkill, together with such soldiers as died in the church during its occupancy as a Conti-nental hospital. No stones marked these burials, and until forty or fifty years ago graves dug to receive the remains of communicants of the parish upturned scraps of blankets, with por-tions of skeletons, revealing the last resting places of some forgotten patriots. Among the modern graves there is also that of Gulian C. Ver Planck, who has been notably identified with the literature of our country and to whose credit an edition of Shakespeare remains.

Trinity Protestant Episcopal Church of Fishkill bears the distinction of being the first edifice erected by the Church of England in Dutchess County, New York, and is still one of the prosperous parishes in that section of the State.

SAN JOSÉ De GUADALUPE

SAN JOSÉ, CALIFORNIA

BEFORE the building of the Roman Catholic Mission of San José the Spanish Missions in California might have been characterised as individual, since each was an isolated unit of civilisation. With the establishment of the Mission at San José, however, close to those of Santa Clara and Soledad, a new era began. In this effort the Spanish padres joined hands with the military authorities to produce peace in the territory lying west of the Rocky Mountains so that the Spanish army there might be reduced. The Spanish Viceroy agreed to contribute a thousand dollars for the establishment of the Mission, provided no increase of troops should be asked for its defence.

On June 12, 1787, the actual work of building the church was begun; timber was cut and water provided, and in a few weeks the simply constructed little buildings were ready for occupancy. The church edifice was of logs, with a grass roof.

The Indians in the vicinity of San José Valley did not seem at all pleased with this broaden-

ing out of the cordon of Missions, but no open
act of hostility occurred until January, 1805,
when Padre Cueva, who was in charge of the
San José Mission, set out to visit a sick convert
some twelve or fifteen miles distant.   His escort
consisted of three Spanish guards and a few
neophytes. The little party rode into an am-
buscade, and the padre and one of his guard
were wounded, while the rest of the party were
killed and their horses captured. The one remaining member of the guard managed to make
his way back to the Mission and word was at once
sent to the Spanish garrison at San Francisco.
A force was quickly sent out, the fleeing hostiles
were overtaken, eleven of them killed, and the
remaining thirty made captives. A tour of investigation that followed during the month of
February disclosed only penitent and submissive
Indians.

The situation of the Mission was most admir-
ably chosen, and so greatly did it prosper that
within eight years after its establishment new
and substantial buildings had been erected from
brick made and baked in the immediate vicinity.
On April 23, 1809, the new Mission Church was
consecrated and the following July the little
cemetery was blessed.

Hostile Indians again attacked the Mission in
1817, carrying off a number of cattle. An
armed force once more set out in pursuit, follow-

St. Joseph's, San José, California

ing a trail which led to a marshy island in the San Joaquin River, where a large body of Indians was concealed. So desperate a fight ensued that for some little time the Spanish leader, Soto, was doubtful of the result. Eventually, however, the Indian ranks broke and they fled for safety, leaving many wounded and dead, but no captives.

By 1824 the Mission of San José had about eighteen hundred communicants, and financially was fourth among the Spanish Missions on the Western frontier. On account of its proximity to the route usually followed by trappers and fugitives from justice, it had a more exciting history than many others. In 1826 there issued from its walls an expedition against the Cosummes in which forty Indians were killed, their rancheria destroyed and a number of captives taken. In 1829 occurred the famous campaign against Estanislas, who had previously so won the confidence of the Spanish missionaries as to be appointed alcalde. Backsliding, he had left the Mission in 1827, accompanied by a large following, and for two years had terrorised the neighbourhood. When he learned of the advance against him of the people of San José Mission, and the Spanish soldiery, he retired to the cover of a dense forest, and the Spanish leader Vallejo, realising that he could make no headway by following the usual military tactics against such an enemy, sent out squads of men, as soon as night had fallen, to fire the woods at different points. Investigation next day proved the wisdom of this course, for the Indians had fled from the widespread conflagration. As soon as the hot embers permitted, the Spaniards followed the trail of the Indians, who, upon being overtaken, still maintained a dogged hostility, but under the persuasion of the cannon that the Spanish trained upon Estanislas they soon surrendered. That the Spanish made an example of the ringleaders in order to quench any lurking desire to follow the example of this renegade, Spanish writers have repeatedly denied, but when one considers the character of the Spanish soldiery he will accept such statements with many a grain of allowance.

In 1826 Jedediah Smith, of Mormon fame, came from the Great Salt on an exploring expedition, but meeting with a cold reception at the hands of the San José padre, he returned to Salt Lake City, being the first white man whose crossing of the Sierras is recorded.

With the separation of the church from the state in 1737, or as the phrase was then, the " secularisation of the Missions," an inventory of the possessions of the Mission of San José de Guadalupe ascribed to it one hundred and fifty-five thousand dollars' worth of property. On March 29, 1843, the Spanish padres were once more placed in possession of the Mission, where they still maintain services regularly. In 1884 a new and modern structure was built for a seminary for novices studying for the priesthood. Later this was placed in charge of the Dominican Sisterhood to be used as an orphan asylum, and as such it is still conducted.

Among the relics in the possession of the Mission are two of the bells that hung in the first old Mission Church; these date back to 1815 and 1826; the timbers upon which they are swung are tied together with rawhide. The old baptismal font too is still used; this is of hammered copper, about three feet in diameter and is surmounted by an iron cross some eight inches in height. The font stands upon a simple wooden upright.

From similarity of name many gather the impression that the Mission is situated in the city of San José; such, however, is not the case, for the Mission buildings and lands lie some little distance from the town, over the foothills toward San Francisco Bay.

ST. PETER'S CHURCH

ALBANY, NEW YORK

THE first American service of the Established Church of England was held in Albany, New York, in 1704, though not in any regularly built or dedicated edifice. Like many another body of Colonial worshippers, for a number of years the communicants could not afford a church of their own, or even a rector. From 1712 to 1715 the Albany Episcopalians worshipped in a little Lutheran church that was kind enough to open its doors to them. It was General Hunter, who had been sent over by Queen Anne to succeed Lord Lovelace as Governor of New York, who at last encouraged them to erect a church of their own, himself contributing a site as well as the stone for the building. Under his influence no doubt many of the officers of the British garrison stationed at Albany added their quota to the expense.

In November, 1715, this first English Church in Albany was dedicated. The building was of stone measuring fifty by forty-two feet. A short tower was added in 1750, and a bell which still bears the date of 1750 was set up in it. The

St. Peter's, Albany, New York

main entrance was toward the south, another
door which led out of the north side of the
building being seldom used. Over the altar, on
the east side, was a triple window, while on both
the north and the south sides were two windows.
The pulpit and reading desk stood between the
two north windows, while the gallery was on the
west side of the building. The interior walls of
the church were adorned with large paintings of
Scriptural scenes, and in one place with the coat
of arms of Great Britain. The communion service was a gift of Queen Anne to " the little
Chapel of the Onondagas," and a handsome
brass clock was also sent over from the old land
for use in the little church.

During the years that elapsed between 1763-6,
the task of translating the Book of Common
Prayer into the Mohawk language was success-
fully accomplished, although not more than
from four to five hundred copies were printed
and bound. In 1758 Lord Howe was killed in
the battle of Ticonderoga, and so highly was he
esteemed in Albany that he was buried under the
chancel of St. Peter's, where his grave is marked
to this day.

In 1790 stoves were introduced for heating
the church, regarded though they were as a great
extravagance by many in the little community of
Albany.

The old church at last became too small to

accommodate the growing membership and was
therefore demolished. A new and more commodious building was dedicated on April 26,
1802. To this edifice were transferred the bell
and the brass clock, both of which were still in
excellent condition. Only twenty years later it
was found necessary to substitute a new and
more modern timepiece, and the brass clock was
preserved as a memento until it was destroyed
in the great fire that swept Albany in 1848.

The third church edifice built by the parishioners of St. Peter's was dedicated in 1859, and is
still occupied regularly for worship. So many
missionaries have gone out from this parish,
founding other churches in various sections of
New York, that St. Peter's may well be regarded
as a mother church of Episcopalians throughout
the State.

FIRST DUTCH REFORMED CHURCH

FISHKILL, NEW YORK

FROM the date of the organisation of the parish of the First Dutch Reformed Church of Fishkill, New York, in the beginning of the eighteenth century, regular services were held from house to house among the members, who, conjointly with two other rural settlements—Hopewell and New Hackensack—were served by a minister of their own faith. The first structure erected by the congregation, a rude and simple affair architecturally, gladdened the hearts of the little flock as one step further in the material kingdom of Christ. The plain walls of logs and the homemade but substantial furnishings found favour in their sight.

This church served the needs of the congregation until 1731, when they built a stone church having unusually liberal dimensions for that day, and place. There was also a tower at the front, with a belfry and steeple. A gallery was built around three sides and the pews were simple and conveniently arranged.

The little community prospered, and as it increased in numbers the Dutch Reformed Church received new members into its communion. The records of the church, which were for a long time accurately kept, were with the death of its secretary some seventy-five years ago unfortunately lost, and found again only after twenty years stored away carefully in the secretary's garret. They had been kept in Dutch, but translations have been made into English and they are regarded as among the most exact and complete of any church records in New York State.

With the breaking out of the Revolution, many recruits were obtained from among the communicants of the Reformed Dutch Church, for its members were as a unit in their patriotism. They promptly offered the use of the church building for representatives of the thirteen Colonies to meet in to consider ways and means for furthering the cause against Great Britain; and the Provincial Convention was held there in 1776. As hostilities extended throughout Eastern New York, Western Connecticut and Massachusetts, the church also served the Continental army as a military prison. It was this prison in which Enoch Crosby—the original from whom Fenimore Cooper drew his character of Harvey Birch—was confined, and from which he made his escape by climbing through the upper portion of a window and springing from the window sill into the branches of a tree that grew close by; for the church stands in a locality generally made famous by the great American novelist.

After the close of the war the church building was restored to its original condition, and enlarged to increase its capacity. No less than three times during the past century—1804, 1820, and 1882—material alterations have been made in the interior finishing and furnishings. The little church is still regularly occupied for service, and its financial as well as its spiritual condition have ever given cause for rejoicing among its communicants.

CHRIST CHURCH

PHILADELPHIA, PENNSYLVANIA

IN North Second Street, Philadelphia, near Market Street, is Christ Church, first among the churches of our country in its associations with the struggle of the Colonies for independence. The present building was erected in 1727-37 in the style of St. Martin's-in-the-Fields, London, and its organisation dates almost from the founding of the colony.

The old church is solidly built, of bricks that were brought from England. In 1754 a chime of bells was purchased in the mother country, the money to pay for them having been raised by a lottery conducted by Benjamin Franklin. There were eight bells in all brought to Philadelphia on the good ship *Myrtilla,* the captain of which declined any compensation for the service. For many years after they had been hung in the belfry, they were rung at noon daily to please the citizens of Philadelphia, as well in the evening before each market day for the gratification of the farmers who had brought their produce to town. The interest shown by all citizens of the City of Brotherly Love in those

Christ Church, Philadelphia, Pennsylvania

bells, irrespective of sect, was great and curious, and indeed they were only the second set of chimes to be imported into the Colonies.

In addition to the regular ringings, the bells were rung on every occasion, important or trifling. When news of disaster was received their tones were muffled and thus carried the tidings to all the townspeople. On July 4, 1776, on the other hand, they rang out loudly and spread the message far and near that the Declaration of Independence had been signed in Independence Hall not far away.

In token of the Christ Church vestry's full approval of the Declaration the bust of King George III. was removed from the prominent niche it had hitherto occupied, an act which was followed a few months later by the destruction of the crown in the spire of the church by lightning. Tory and Loyalist no doubt looked upon this circumstance as an omen.

On July 20, 1775, Congress attended service in Christ Church in a body. Under its roof too was perfected the organisation of the Episcopal Church in America, a convention having been called for the purpose in 1785. Treasured among the archives of the parish is an original copy of the Prayer Book of Edward VI., with alterations made in the convention in accordance with the proposed act of disruption from the Church of England.

General Washington attended service at Christ Church from 1790 to 1797 and the pew he occupied is preserved in the National Museum in Washington; another pew is also preserved —that occupied by Betsy Ross, who made the first American flag.

The old church is rich in treasures, including ancient volumes, furniture, tablets and silver vessels, many of them possessing extreme historic interest.

THE OLD DUTCH CHURCH

TARRYTOWN, NEW YORK

CLOSELY linked with the Revolutionary history of Tarrytown is the old Dutch Church built there near the close of the seventeenth century.

Early in the history of the New Netherlands a youth named Vredyk Flypse, a Bohemian by birth, came over from Holland to New Amsterdam. His sole capital consisted in his trade of carpentry, and that he soon abandoned for the more lucrative pursuit of dealing in furs. Not long afterward his marriage with the widow of one of the most successful fur traders in New Netherlands made him, for those days, a man of considerable wealth. In 1680 Meinheer Flypse obtained a grant of certain tracts of land situated in the county of Westchester and extending from Spuyten Duyvil along the Hudson River as far north as the Kill of Kitch Awong. Within three years after obtaining this grant, Vredyk Flypse had erected for himself a manor house, a mill and a little church on the Pocantico that is still in existence and most highly cherished by the people of Tarrytown, as well as by all residents of New York State who are aware of its interest. The bricks used in the construction of the chimney of the church, were brought from Holland in vessels owned and operated by Meinheer Flypse, as was also the church bell. With true commercial instinct, the old burgher had established a substantial trade between New Amsterdam and England and Holland, shipping furs to Europe and importing various commodities that found ready sale in New Netherlands, and the bricks and bell came over in his ships.

The construction of the Pocantico Church, as well as that of the manor house, was ponderous enough to suggest that they were meant to endure as monuments of their builder for all time. The church walls were thirty inches thick, and the windows in them were elevated seven feet above the ground and had iron bars to serve the better for protection against hostile Indians. Within the church a huge pulpit, with a broad sounding-board, projected from the eastern wall. Originally, the seats for the congregation were without backs, for the purpose of forbidding lounging or slumber during the sermon, in naïve contrast with the comfortable and imposing pews that, ranged on either side of the pulpit, provided agreeable seats for the occupants of the manor house and their notable visitors. The farmers who resided near by occupied the body of the church, while a gallery served for slaves and for " Redemptioners," poor settlers who had sold their services for a time to pay the cost of their passage from the Old World.   Within the church still stands the ancient bier, around which many tears have no doubt been shed since the dedication of the edifice in 1697 by the Reverend Guiliam Berthoff, who came from Holland specially to serve the little community.

During the stormy days of the Revolution the church was closed, and so strong did the spirit of liberty and equality rage in the parish that the trappings that had distinguished the pew of the lord of the manor were torn down and burned. Thereafter, this pew and its fellows were appropriated by the elders and deacons of the church, an act indicative of the triumph of democratic ideas in church and state.

No rural church in our country has gained so wide a fame as this little Dutch Reformed Church in Sleepy Hollow.   In its modest graveyard lie the remains of that gentle humourist, Washington Irving, whose intense love for this locality and the little church itself has imbued many readers with affection and reverence for it. The two hundredth anniversary of the dedication of the church brought together from all sections of the country men of every denomination, who hastened to join hands in its memory, as well as to render homage to the great writer whose love for the old edifice was so deep and lasting.

ST. PAUL'S CHURCH

NORFOLK, VIRGINIA

AMONG the old churches of the South, both architecturally and in point of history, few are more interesting than St. Paul's Protestant Episcopal Church, of Norfolk, Virginia.

Raised bricks set in its wall testify to 1739 as the date of the church's erection, very soon after the establishment of the first settlement there, and the granting of a charter by act of the Virginia Assembly. In plan the building is cruciform, and the doors are arched in accordance with the prevailing custom of those times, while the beauty of the windows still arouses admiration.

During the Revolution the old church, as well as its church property, suffered much. Its rector at that date was the Reverend Thomas Davis, whose sympathies were wholly with the American colonists, and who, in 1766, was chairman of a well-attended town meeting to protest against the notorious Stamp Act. This action was not forgotten by the British ten years later when their army bombarded Norfolk, under Lord

St. Paul's, Norfolk, Virginia

Dunmore, and entirely destroyed the city. Nothing remained of the little church of St. Paul's except the walls, in one of which, the south wall, a cannon ball still bears witness of the British onslaught.

After the close of the Revolution St. Paul's was rebuilt, in the original plan, using the original walls. The same contour was followed in the doorways, and the quaint old windows also were replaced. Its career has been signally successful, and from time to time St. Paul's has planted offshoots here and there, until the churches that have grown up under her protection number at least ten.

St. Paul's lay in the track of the contending armies during the great Civil War; each army, North or South, in turn occupied it, and the close of the war found it devastated, its communicants dead or scattered, and its treasury depleted. It was only as the years rolled on that the congregation gradually gathered up its courage once more and repaired the church building. Although certain improvements were added, the original lines were again faithfully preserved, as they had been after the Revolution, and to-day the church bids fair to stand for another two hundred years of activity and energy.

St. Paul's churchyard is regarded as the most beautiful cemetery in all Virginia. Among those who lie there are many who fought both for and against the United States as a nation, not only during the Revolution, but the Civil War as well. Here also are found the graves of the original Huguenots who first settled in Virginia, together with those of many men whose forefathers bore an honourable part in the history of Scotland and Ireland.

FIRST DUTCH REFORMED CHURCH

FLATBUSH, LONG ISLAND

IMMEDIATELY following the settlement of Manhattan Island various pioneers, casting a look ahead and attracted by the promised profits of farming on Long Island, pre-empted land on the opposite side of the East River, and began to live there. These settlers, regarding themselves as part and parcel of the greater settlement, may, indeed, be looked upon as the progenitors of " Greater New York." For almost twenty years they travelled over to Manhattan to worship in the little church building within the fort, served by theological students sent out by the West India Company, who recognised the American colony as humble members of the Synod of Holland and the Classis of Amsterdam. The name given these lay readers was " Comforters of the Sick," and occasionally when service was conducted in the house or barn of some invalid communicant, the settlers for miles inland attended *en masse*.

In 1628 the first regularly ordained minister of the Gospel, Domine Michaelius, was sent out to the American Colony by the North Synod

of Holland.   Upon his arrival he organised the
first body of the Reformed Dutch Church in
America, embodying some fifty communicants.
Three years later he was followed by Domine
Everardus Bogardus.   The year of his advent
into the American Church organisation, 1633,
was marked by the erection of the first regular
church building of the Dutch Reformed Church
in America.

As the Long Island settlers prospered, they
decided that they, too, were able to erect a church
of their own.   They had been dependent upon
the rudest sort of methods for crossing the East
River, their ferry consisting merely of a small
flat-boat rowed by some nearby farmer, who was
summoned by a horn which hung conveniently on
a neighbouring tree for the purpose.   The length
of the passage depended upon the weather and
tide, and the ancient Long Islanders decided it
was time they should make their church-going
less hazardous.

In 1654 they accordingly completed the erection of their first house of worship.   They
selected Flatbush as the most central and convenient site for the residents of " Breukelen, Med-
wont and Amersfort "—as Brooklyn, Flatbush
and Flatlands were then called.   The cost of the
building was eighteen hundred dollars, to which
fund Governor Peter Stuyvesant, the last Dutch
" Director-General " of the New Netherlands,

contributed liberally. It was in the form of a cross, sixty-five feet long by twenty-eight feet wide, and from twelve to fourteen feet from floor to ceiling. In architectural style and in interior finish the church was plain and simple, being thoroughly characteristic of the homely life led by these Dutch burghers.

The communicants of the Dutch Church were most emphatic in demanding broad and thorough theological training in the ministers sent out to serve them. Of these the Reverend Johannus Theodorus Polhemus was the first regularly ordained minister at Flatbush. Under his preaching the church prospered, and in 1681 had attained so great a prominence in the New Netherlands Classis that the consistory of the church was enlarged by the addition of still another deacon, selected from the communicants who resided at New Lots. For many years none of the Dutch Reformed churches on Long Island, with the exception of the church at Flatbush, had more than two elders and two deacons.

The number of worshippers increased duly, and in 1698 arrangements were made to erect a new church edifice. The communicants wished, moreover, to possess a building in which they could take some pride. To one of the leading elders is attributed the remark that they were ashamed to have the English see them attending service in a mean church building, since the first thing that

New Englanders did, after erecting places of shelter for their families, was to build a substantial church. Accordingly the Dutch at Flatbush at once started a subscription for a building fund, and before a great while accumulated something over six thousand dollars—a large sum for those times. No record exists of contributions being asked from any outside the communicants of the church, nor did any debt remain to be liquidated by later members, two facts which testify to the prosperous condition of the little Dutch colony.

The location selected for the new church was the site of the old building, and the stones of the old church were again employed in the foundation of the new structure. The entire edifice was of stone, with its front facing the east, in which a large, arched, double door opened. The roof was steep, rising from each of the four walls, and at its apex a small steeple was built, in which was hung a bell brought from Holland. The building was wider in its front than its depth, being sixty-five feet from north to south, while it measured only fifty feet from east to west. The roof rested partly upon the walls and partly upon two large oaken columns which stood within the church equi-distant from each other and from the nearest wall. These two columns supported a plate in the centre of the lofty, arched, plank ceiling, while the north and south ends of the roof rested upon the walls.

The consequence was that these end walls were higher than the east and west walls. To make the roof more secure, the two interior oak supports were braced together heavily. This unusual construction was most defective, as may be supposed, for the pressure was so great upon the north and south walls that in time the upper portion of the north wall was forced more than a foot out of plumb.

The pulpit stood in the centre of the west side of the building, and at its right were the seats for the elders of the church, and at its left, those for the deacons. The male portion of the congregation was provided with seats along the walls on three sides of the church, while the centre was devoted to the use of the women. The women and little girls occupied chairs, the men and boys unpretentious benches, divided into twenty compartments with low doors. The chairs were ranged in seven rows or blocks, and each was marked upon the back with the name of the owner. The windows were formed of small panes of glass, those on each side of the pulpit being painted, or ornamented with lead mullions.

In 1775 the seating arrangements of the church were changed and pews to the number of sixty-four substituted for the chairs and benches. Each pew provided for the seating of at least six people, and families were again reunited in the church sittings. A short gallery was also built on each side of the entrance door, one of them reserved for the use of communicants who were too poor to pay the rental of a pew, the other for coloured members. Conspicuous in their location and finish were two pews near the pulpit in the front of the body of the church. In one of these sat the minister's family, and in the other any notable visitors that might come for worship. In a prominent position near the pulpit hung a board upon which was regularly noted the Psalms to be sung during service each Sunday.

The old Psalm books carried to church and used during the service deserve mention. Each was curiously bound in silver at the corners and was fastened by ornamental clasps. Attached to the Psalm book by a silver ring were long cords or silver chains with which to hang it at the back of the chair during the sermon. The Psalms of David and the New Testament were bound together in the Dutch "Psalm books," some of which have been preserved to this day by descendants of the original church members.

Though no provision whatever was made for heating the church, ample means was supplied for arousing the settlement in the event of Indian attacks. The bell rope which descended from the belfry down through the middle aisle of the church, was rung not only to call the congregation together for worship, but also to warn the settlers when an attack threatened. During the Revolution, when the British landed on Long Island in August, 1776, the bell in the Flatbush Dutch Reformed Church sounded the first alarm.

After the Battle of Long Island the British carried their wounded into the Flatbush Church, which became temporarily a hospital. When other quarters for the sick and wounded were provided later the church served the British artillery as a stable for their horses. The whole interior was demolished, and the pews built only the year previous were burnt as fuel or to cook the soldiers' rations. At the end of the war, when the British troops had quitted Long Island, the surviving communicants of the Flatbush Reformed Dutch Church got together again and undertook the renovation of the building. They seem to have felt, however, that their house of worship had been contaminated by the uses to which it had been put by the British, and in 1793 decided to build a new church. The old building was torn down, and a new church erected on its site. The stone which had entered into the construction of the first two churches was again used in building the new foundations. Small Dutch bricks to be placed around the doors and windows were imported from Holland, and the brown stone used in the construction of the edifice above the foundation walls was quarried from the rocky ridge that lies between Flatbush and Brooklyn. Limestone to complete the foundations was obtained from the quarries of " Hell Gate." The cost of the church edifice was about twelve thousand dollars, exclusive of much labour and cartage, which were contributed by the communicants of the church. In January, 1797, the consecration sermon was delivered in the Dutch language by Domine Schoonmaker. Since 1792 services had been conducted in English and in Dutch on alternate Sabbaths, but after the death of Domine Schoonmaker in 1824, at the age of ninety years, the use of the Dutch language was discontinued. The Domine's body was buried under the church, as were those of all ministers who died in office, and of the earlier communicants as well. This custom accounts for the lack of early dates upon the gravestones in the little cemetery around the church. In one portion of this graveyard, where there is a total absence of gravestones, those who were killed in the Battle of Long Island were hurriedly buried. As haste was necessary, no coffins or headstones were used. To the memory of these soldiers this section of the graveyard was considered consecrated and no later burials have taken place therein.

The church is still used regularly for service each Sabbath. In 1836 the high-backed pews gave place to more modern seats, the grained

woodwork was painted white, and two cast iron
stoves were introduced to heat the building. The
pulpit was of mahogany, erected on a pedestal
five or six feet above the level of the floor, and
reached by a winding staircase. In 1836 blinds
were furnished for the first time and the aisles
and pulpit provided with their first carpet.
Later, in 1862, the high pulpit gave place to one
more modern and the two stoves to a furnace.
An organ was installed and a clock placed in the
steeple. By an ingenious contrivance this clock
strikes upon the old bell presented to the church
in 1796 by the Honourable John Vanderbilt, who
imported it from Holland in one of his merchant
vessels. During its voyage, by the way, this vessel was captured by a British man-of-war and
detained for some time at Halifax, so that the
bell finally reached its proper destination by a
roundabout route. In 1887 the members again
altered and refurnished the church. A door was
built in the rear wall to accommodate the minister, and a robing room was added for his use.
The interior walls were stencilled in quiet colours,
and new upholstery and carpets were provided to
harmonise with the new walls. An addition was
also built for the new and larger organ that was
purchased, and in 1890 stained glass windows
were introduced. Many of these were gifts in
memory of the pioneer families that organised
the First Reformed Dutch Church of Flatbush.

THE MORAVIAN CHURCH

BETHLEHEM, PENNSYLVANIA

SHAKESPEARE'S remark that some men are born great, others achieve greatness and others have greatness thrust upon them is equally applicable to localities. No denomination of Christians are less seekers for notoriety than the Moravians, yet in the history of our country the town of Bethlehem, Pennsylvania, with its little Moravian church, has won fame from its association with the names of Lafayette and Pulaski.

It has been claimed by historians that the Moravians constitute the oldest existing Protestant church, dating their origin from the days of John Huss. Driven by persecution from one hiding place to another, they settled in 1722 upon the estates of Count Zinzendorf in Saxony, founding the historic town of Herrnhut. The Count, although a strict Lutheran, became deeply interested in their religious views, and finally accepting their belief he was advanced to the position of Bishop in the Moravian Church.

One of the chief functions of these early Moravians was the establishment of missions in

Moravian Church, Bethlehem, Pennsylvania

various sections of the world for the teaching of
the religion of Jesus Christ, as they understood
it.   It was therefore natural that they should
cast their eyes toward America, where the be-
nighted might learn the way of salvation.   In
1740 they purchased a large tract of land in the
eastern section of Pennsylvania, naming the city
they founded there Bethlehem.   The following
year Count Zinzendorf came over, and through
his efforts numerous missions sprang up for the
enlightenment of the Indians.   At Bethlehem
the chapel house, the Bishop's house, and the
residence of the Moravian Sisterhood were clustered upon the original tract of land.   The
dedication of the famous chapel took place on
September 19, 1742, and the first convert to be
buried in the graveyard attached to the chapel
was an Indian.   Previous to the erection of this
chapel, religious service was held in a large room
on the second floor of " das gemein Haus "
which they termed " der Saal "—the entertainment room in the home of the Brotherhood.

On April 5, 1751, the population of the town
had increased to such numbers that the small
chapel proved inadequate and a large room was
annexed to the " Old Chapel."   In this addition
the first floor was set apart for the married members of the Moravian community, while the upper
floor was used as chapel.   The organ that had
been built in the old chapel was removed to the

new, and there the voices of the "Moravian Nuns" blended with the notes of the organ in the worship of God.

The establishment in the community of one of the best conducted hospitals that America could then boast of brought many strangers to their doors. This hospital was under the special care of the Moravian Sisterhood, and thither, on one occasion came General Lafayette to have his wound cared for; and to this same community came Count Pulaski, who had been assigned to protect it against incursions by hostile British and Indians. Accompanying Count Pulaski (or Polowsky, as his name appears in the records of the community) was Colonel Koabatsch, "a Prussian officer of Huzzars who had been living in retirement," and who was engaged in organising a troop of cavalry for Continental service. From all accounts he gathered many a recruit from the younger members of the community, for the records of the Moravians announce the departure of Colonel Koabatsch, "with his troopers, armed and equipped, on July 31, 1778."

On May 15 Pulaski is mentioned in these same records as having attended service in the chapel with some of his staff, in stately array. From that service he carried with him the banner which the poet Longfellow has immortalised in his poem, "The Hymn of the Moravian Nuns."

This banner, a silk guidon embroidered by the sisters, Pulaski bore fluttering from an upright lance at the head of his legions, until he fell at Savannah in October, 1779. This banner, also, which was preserved by the comrades of Count Pulaski with religious care, was carried in the procession that welcomed Lafayette upon his visit to this country in 1824, and was later presented to the Maryland Historical Society, in whose possession it has remained since 1844.

The sentiment that prompted the giving of the banner has never been fully revealed, but so long as the history of our country's struggle shall be told and the names of her European allies mentioned, the kindly spirit of the Moravian Community who cared for the sick of the Continental troops and provided liberally for the welfare of the American patriots will be gratefully remembered.

"OLD JERUSALEM"

PORTLAND, MAINE

THE old First Church of Portland, Maine, in its organisation, dates from the first settlement of the town, although the members were for a number of years too poor to build a meeting-house. In 1720 they got as far as putting up the framework of a building, though still with no funds available for the support of a pastor. This first building was used by fishermen and soldiers as a barracks, until the Reverend Thomas Smith came to the settlement in 1725, and it was decided to complete and occupy the church. Governor Wentworth contributed the glass for the windows, and a church was at last finished and painted.

A second and more substantial church was built some years later, and on July 20, 1740, was dedicated to the worship of God. The first old structure became the property of the town and was used for civic purposes until it burned down in 1775. The new edifice was a formidable-looking pile, painted white, with green trimmings. Over the minister's head hung the inevitable huge sounding-board, suspended by a wooden rod from a pineapple carved in the rafters. Such massive timbers of white oak were employed in the construction of the church as to arouse the opinion that the builder was more accustomed to build boats than meeting-houses, and thought it necessary to provide against fierce storms. The new church had its first bell in 1758, imported especially, and mounted on a special framework. When the news of the closing of Boston Harbour in 1774 reached Portland, this same old bell tolled for twenty-four hours, joined in its rite of sadness by every other church bell in the little city. From that day to this the bell of the First Church is invariably waited for on all occasions, the others joining in the ringing after her first peal is heard.

As the members of the congregation increased in numbers the old building grew too small to accommodate them, and a meeting was called to consider what had best be done. In view of the substantial character of the meeting-house they decided that it would be more economical to enlarge it than to erect a new one. Following these deliberations they had the end of the meeting-house nearest the bell sawed off, with its supports, and extended the side walls so that when the end was again attached it reached the supports of the bell, which had before stood independently. The whole structure was then encased with boards, so that the framework supporting the bell formed a tower at the end of the church, and was converted into the front entrance.   A rededication of the edifice took place in 1761, when the alterations were finished.

The old church has had its times of war as well as of peace, and long bore the marks of them.   Naturally the exposed position of Portland as a seaport made her liable to attack from the British, and during one bombardment a cannon ball from Mowatt's fleet passed through the outer walls and lodged inside the building.   This ball was preserved carefully, and when the present church was erected in 1825, was embedded in the centre of the ceiling.   From it was suspended the large chandelier of the older church, which lights the congregation still, the building erected in 1825 being still occupied regularly for services.

In 1821 a special service was held in the First Church for the large number of sailors and seafaring folk that inhabited the old city of Portland, and the church was packed as it had never been before.   It was upon this occasion that it was given the appellation " Old Jerusalem," as which it has ever since been known.

ST. PAUL'S

EAST CHESTER, NEW YORK

THE original English settlers in Westchester County, New York, seem to have
provided without delay for their spiritual
needs. As early as 1665 such arrangements
were made as secured to them the services of a
rector, who watched over three or four parishes,
none of them being sufficiently wealthy to pay
for the exclusive services of a rector of its own.

In 1692 it was decided to erect a church building in East Chester, which was completed in
1700. So closely allied at that time were church
and state in New York that the consent of the
Governor was asked for the induction of a rector
into this little parish. This being refused, an
application was made to the "General Assembly" of the State for permission to separate
from the parish, which had till then embodied
Westchester, Pelham, Yonkers and New Ro-
chelle. This was granted in an act of the
Legislature establishing East Chester as an independent religious State organisation, with the
name of "the Parish of East Chester." This
Act was not, however, approved by the Bishop

of London, and by order of Queen Anne was disallowed.

The little church building erected in 1700 is described as a frame building, twenty-eight feet square, about eighteen feet to the eaves, the sides of the building, as well as the roof, being covered with shingles. The building stood on the " Green," and to-day is still discernible among such ancient trees as have endured the ravages of time.

Gradually the number of communicants increased, until in 1787 East Chester became an independent parish. In 1795, under the provisions of an act for the relief and maintenance of the Protestant Episcopal Church in America, the parish was reorganised, according to the rulings which separated the Church in America from the Established Church of England, and then for the first time the parish in East Chester took the name of St. Paul.

By 1764 the little old chapel had so far succumbed to the elements as to be too cold for worship in winter, despite the piety of the early fathers. The foundations of a new church building were laid. Services in the meantime were conducted in the old building until October, 1776, when the new church was completed.

During the War of the Revolution, the new church building was used as a hospital for the British, who tore portions of it down from time

St. Paul's, East Chester, New York

to time and used them as fuel. Fortunately the church authorities had been clever enough to bury the bell and the communion service, which were thus preserved from the enemy. Four years after the close of the war the services were resumed, and have continued till the present day.

The churchyard about St. Paul's is closely connected with the history of the church. In its three and one-half acres it holds over six thousand bodies. The oldest inscription legible bears the date of 1704. The churchyard is surrounded by a substantial wall, in which are incorporated the vaults of the older members of the parish. Among those whose remains rest in East Chester churchyard may be found men whose names have been well known in commercial circles in New York City, as well as officers both of the Continental troops and of the British soldiery who died in the hospital.

FIRST CONGREGATIONAL CHURCH

SALEM, MASSACHUSETTS

THE first Congregational Church organised in North America was formed in Salem, Massachusetts, in July and August of the year 1627. Only freed men were eligible as members, and from 1627 to 1634 services were held in a humble and unfinished building. In 1634 the members got together some money, and began the erection of a suitable house of worship, which, however, was not wholly completed till 1639. Even then many portions of it were so poorly built that for twelve years later considerable repairs were still called for. The meeting-house had a thatched roof, and the walls were daubed with clay and mud, shingles and clapboards being too expensive to be thought of. The pulpit, of a style round in shape like a tub, was raised high on a platform, on the steps of which, as well as upon the two flights of the steps that led to the gallery, the boys of the congregation sat during worship. Sentinels trod back and forward across the " Green " during church time, doing double service, on the lookout for Indian foes, and watchful lest any member leave the church before service was over.

This primitive meeting-house gave place in 1670 to one more in accord with the increased prosperity of the congregation. The new building stood upon a tract of land donated by the town, at the western end of the plot upon which the old church had stood, and "looking toward the prison." The old building was then used for a schoolhouse and watchhouse, and with "Yankee thrift" the old pulpit and the deacon's seats were divided among the farmers and put to practical uses in their homes. The steady increase in the membership of the church rendered this newer building also unequal to the task of seating the congregation, and by 1718 a still more commodious and substantial structure was in course of erection. This third structure was occupied for one hundred and eight years.

The First Congregational Church of Salem was not so happy in its career as to be without a history. Internal dissension split the congregation into two parties, liberal and conservative, eighteen years after the third building was put up. So partisan did these two sides become and so high did the ill-feeling mount that actual riots took place between the opposing factions, and it is even on record that the conservative element on one occasion publicly "arraigned and admonished " one member of the congregation, together with his wife. The progressive faction split off indeed finally from the old church, and erected a new edifice not eighteen yards from the old building, where they worshipped according to their own lights.

As time went by this fierce spirit was, of course, gradually modified and peace restored. The present brick building, now occupied by the inheritors of the original congregation, was dedicated in 1826, and contains within its walls many relics of the older structures.

THE MORMON TABERNACLE AND TEMPLE

SALT LAKE CITY, UTAH

PERHAPS no church in America is more extraordinary in point of architectural achievement or religious history than the great Mormon Tabernacle at Salt Lake City. The founder of the Mormons, with their doctrine of plurality of wives, Joseph Smith, born in the State of Vermont in 1805, and from an early age receiving, as he claimed, "visions" that ranged from the dreams of Joan of Arc to revelations such as the tablets of stone and the burning, fiery furnace of the Old Testament, laid the groundwork of a sect which was to enjoy material prosperity and has left a landmark in the huge "temple" in Utah.

Joseph Smith's first attempt to found his Mormon Church was in 1830 in New York City. The opposition which was to meet him everywhere soon compelled him to seek some other locality. Through Ohio, where a "temple" was erected, and on to Missouri he led his increasing following, planting a colony at Jackson. There had also been a Mormon colony which prospered for a time on Beaver Island in Lake Michigan. Popular prejudice, however, compelled them to abandon the land whereon they made settlements and to seek an abiding place elsewhere.

Meanwhile missionaries from the Mormon Church were visiting various sections of Europe, and sent to America their first instalment of proselytes in 1840. After the violent death of Joseph Smith, the celebrated Brigham Young became the head of the Church, and under his famous leadership the Mormons continued their exodus westward, seeking some locality where they might live in peace, unmolested by those who believed in only one wife, and whose moral opinions otherwise differed from the principles set forth in the Book of Mormon. In July, 1847, they reached an oasis in the heart of the great American desert, and there founded Salt Lake City, not far from the Great Salt Lake, where Brigham Young had secured from the Mexican government a broad tract of land. They began at once the erection of the great tabernacle and other requisite buildings, but the work proved slow, and they had to put forth herculean efforts in its accomplishment. The timber and stone used in constructing the church, for instance, had to be hauled by oxen from the Cottonwood Cañon, twenty miles away.

The present great Mormon Temple, which is to be distinguished from the Tabernacle, was

Mormon Temple and Tabernacle, Salt Lake City, Utah

built of solid granite brought at an expenditure
of tremendous labour from the Wasatch Mountains, forty to fifty miles distant. Though the
corner stone of the Temple was laid by Brigham
Young on April 6, 1853, it was twenty years
before the building was finished and dedicated.
The cost of this structure is estimated to have
been not less than four million dollars.

Four other temples were erected, but none was
so unusual in design nor so curious as the Tabernacle. The great Tabernacle covers an area of
two hundred and fifty by one hundred and fifty
feet and seats eight thousand people. The colos-
sal arch of the roof springs from wall to wall
supported by forty-four sandstone pillars. The
enormous turtle-backed edifice is impressive certainly if only on account of its size. Within is
the organ—a most noticeable feature, one of the
largest in the country. It was constructed by
Utah artisans from native material, and may well
be regarded as a creditable mechanical and artistic achievement.

In spite of persecution without and frequent
dissensions within, the Church of the Latter Day
Saints has prospered without intermission and
to-day numbers almost half a million followers.
Twelve or fourteen thousand of its missionaries
are scattered throughout Europe.

ST. GEORGE'S

PHILADELPHIA, PENNSYLVANIA

IT is not generally known that the City of Brotherly Love can boast of the oldest house of worship of the Methodist Episcopal Church in America. In other localities where this denomination had its beginnings, the various buildings dedicated to the service of God have gradually been replaced by more modern edifices, leaving St. George's in Philadelphia the oldest existing structure.

To Captain Thomas Webb, an officer in the British army, was due the possession by the Methodists of this house of worship. Captain Webb had been a convert to the preaching of the Reverend John Wesley, the founder of the Methodist Episcopal Church, and from him got a licence as a local preacher. At least as early as 1768 he visited Philadelphia, and preached there in a sail-loft in default of any church building. The owner of the loft, on Dock Street, one Mr. Crofts, was himself a Wesleyan convert.

From this humble meeting-place the congregation soon made a change, and next held services in a house in Loxley's Court, a small thoroughfare running from Arch to Cherry Streets, just below Fourth Street.

On October 21, 1769, two regularly ordained missionaries of the denomination came to Philadelphia—the first missionaries sent by John Wesley to America. One of these, Mr. Joseph Pilmoor, learning of the presence in that city of Members of the Methodist Episcopal Church and of more recent converts, decided to remain and advance the cause of his church in Philadelphia. Still in default of any place of worship Mr. Pilmoor preached in Franklin Square, and on some occasions from the steps of Independence Hall. When the weather forbade outdoor gatherings, the congregation met as heretofore in the room in Loxley's Court, which soon became too small to accommodate the increasing number of those who came to hear "the Word," even on rainy Sundays.

Meanwhile there stood in the city an unoccupied church building, erected by members of the High Dutch Reformed Church, who had been unable to meet their payments on it as they fell due, and in order to satisfy their creditors were ordered by the court to sell the building at auction. The highest bidder, as it happened, was an irresponsible young man of feeble mind, whose father began at once to seek a purchaser who should take off his hands a church structure for which, to all practical intents, he felt that his

son had no use. He succeeded in selling the
property to Mr. Miles Pennington, one of the
most active members of the still embryonic Methodist Episcopal Church, for the same sum of
two thousand six hundred dollars, exclusive of
the land upon which the church stood, the congregation assuming the ground rent of one hundred dollars a year.

This queerly bought structure, fifty-five by
eighty-five feet, was regarded as an unusually
large one at that time. It was consecrated November 24, 1769, the day following the purchase
by Mr. Pennington, who dedicated it to the service of God as a house of worship according to
the customs of the Methodist Episcopal Church.
The building was far from completion, but the
members nevertheless rejoiced over their purchase and gave thanks. The following Sunday,
the dedication having taken place on Friday, the
little structure was crowded to the utmost with
some two thousand people.

At once the members of the church began to
plan for the completion of the structure, which
was for the most part unplastered and only
partly floored, and in every way primitive. During the first winter, foot stoves had to be used
as a means for keeping the people warm during
services.

During the eventful period of the Revolution,
while the British army was in possession of Phila-

delphia, St. George's Church was used as a hospital, and later as a "riding school" for the cavalry; relics of the War were gathered in and about the church in abundance for a long time after America had secured her independence.

The great procession in Philadelphia in 1780 which marked the bitter feeling against Benedict Arnold formed in front of St. George's Church. The first General Conference of the Methodist Episcopal Church in America was held at St. George's, and the Reverend Francis Asbury, the first American Bishop in the denomination, presided. We have it on contemporary authority that he cherished a warm love for this first church of the Methodists in America and returned to it whenever he found it possible. His first sermon in America was preached within its walls.

While other congregations of the same denomination have rebuilt and altered their houses of worship to conform to more modern ideas, St. George's has remained substantially as it was in the beginning—a sacred memento of the past, and perhaps the most ancient land-mark in the whole world of the Methodist Episcopal Church.

ST. MICHAEL'S

CHARLESTON, SOUTH CAROLINA

NO object sooner attracts the attention of persons on board vessels entering the harbour of Charleston, South Carolina, than the steeple of St. Michael's Protestant Episcopal Church. A closer examination discloses the fact that this edifice is one of the best specimens of the art of building exhibited by British constructive talent in America in the eighteenth century. It is one hundred and thirty feet long, including the portico, and sixty feet wide, has an elevation of one hundred and sixty-eight feet, and is of brick, with a slate roof, making a most attractive showing on the sandy slope of the Charleston shore.

At the west end of the building rises a graceful steeple, and at the top of this is a gilt ball, of black cypress, covered with copper, surmounted by a weather vane. During the cyclone of August 25, 1885, this ball was hurled to the ground, making a spherical impression in the heavy flag-stone pavement. Curiously enough the wood was found to be in a perfect state of preservation, and the coating was repaired and

St. Michael's, Charleston, South Carolina

the ball restored to its former position. The tower of the church consists of a series of ornamental chambers, rising gradually one above the other, a style involving greater difficulties of construction than were usually incurred at the period at which the church was built.

The corner stone of the church was laid by the Governor of the State on February 17, 1752, and the church was first opened for divine service on February 1, 1761. The intervening time was not wholly occupied in the construction of the building, but in a great measure by the difficulty of procuring a clergyman acceptable to the parishioners.

Scarcely was the little parish settled in its new church building when it began to plan and contrive to purchase a chime of bells. Three years later, on July 15, 1764, their hearts were rejoiced and their efforts rewarded by the arrival of a ship from England bearing not only the coveted chimes, but also a church clock. No American church has ever possessed a better set of chimes than St. Michael's, which, until the installation of a modern fire alarm system in Charleston in 1882, gave warning from its steeple of all fires in the city.

Since Charleston was the chief city in the Colony, Governor Boone contributed to the furnishing of St. Michael's, giving the parish a silver communion service, engraved with the name of the donor and the date of its presentation to the parish. To these some of the citizens of Charleston added two silver alms dishes and a silver christening bowl. As the years passed, gifts of still other pieces of eucharistic silver augmented the treasures of St. Michael's, until they now excel those of almost any other church in the South.

The next most coveted possession was a church organ, which the parish secured in August, 1768; and on Christmas Eve, 1771, a marble baptismal font was placed in the position which it still occupies.

As in many other communities the breaking out of the War of Independence was the signal for many differences of opinion and dissensions in the church. The rector, a staunch Loyalist, held exasperatingly to the performance of his vows as a clergyman of the Established Church of England, while most of the parishioners, especially the vestrymen, were equally earnest in their desire to revolt absolutely from English rule. This situation resulted finally in a demand for the English rector's resignation.

While the British occupied Charleston during the Revolution ammunition was so scarce that they robbed St. Michael's of its roof to secure lead for bullets. Service was interrupted and no regular rector was secured until July 29, 1781. The church plate, being very valuable, was placed in the keeping of one of the vestry-men, who removed it wholly from Charleston until the war was ended. So closely allied were the church and state at that time that the per-mission of the Governor was considered neces-sary before such precautionary steps were taken.

The communicants of St. Michael's con-tributed generously to the cause of freedom, and as a result the finances of the parish suffered considerably for several years after the close of the war. Since it was unable to support a rec-tor, after the evacuation of the British and the re-entry of the South Carolina regiments, the chaplain of one of these read service regularly in the church for many months. In May, 1785, the two parishes of St. Michael's and St. Philip's were incorporated together. Six years there-after, individual corporations were formed again, and in three years St. Michael's was fully repaired and a parapet built on both the north and the south sides. This latter addition proved inadvisable and was removed in 1847.

So popular was the church that many bodies held meetings within its walls, among them the Free Masons and various Revolutionary soci-ties, the Order of the Cincinnati, and the Pal-metto. When it became evident in 1811 and 1812 that the difficulties between Great Britain and the United States would again lead to war the citizens of Charleston assembled in St.

Michael's to decide in what manner they could best aid the Government in its insistence upon the rights of American citizens.

On Sunday, November 19, 1863, just after the litany had been read, a bomb from the United States batteries at Morris Island exploded at the church door, while still another struck the church steeple. As the bombardment continued the congregation was dismissed without the usual sermon. General Hood's army used the steeple of St. Michael's as a look-out station, suspending a rope ladder from the second balcony to be used in case of a hurried retreat.

As a precautionary measure the organ had been removed from the church, and the bells, at the suggestion of General Beauregard, had been sent to Columbia early in the conflict as a contribution from the church toward supplying metal for casting cannon. Though not used for this purpose, during Sherman's march to the sea they were wantonly broken into many pieces by reckless members of his army. After the close of the Civil War the pieces were carefully gathered together and sent back to London where they were made. There they were recast and finally made their re-entrance into Charleston. They were met with joyful acclamation by members of every religious denomination throughout the city.

Great repairs were necessary after the bombardment of Charleston, in which St. Michael's had received much damage. One end of the chancel had been torn off, pews had been demolished, and to make matters worse curio hunters had broken off and carried away portions of the pulpit and chancel. The church was again open for service on November 26, 1865. Twenty years later the great cyclone that struck Charleston wrecked St. Michael's spire, together with portions of the slate roof. In the following year, on August 31, 1886, the great earthquake occasioned the most serious disaster that St. Michael's church had yet experienced. It shattered the walls in numerous places, threw the spire out of the perpendicular, and sunk it eight inches. The shock also opened a fissure in the church floor several inches wide which ran through the vestibule and up the middle aisle for a distance of ten or twelve feet, while the portico seemed about to topple into the street and the galleries to tumble into the body of the church. At an expense of no less than fifteen thousand dollars the church was finally restored to its original condition, and is still one of the most interesting landmarks in Charleston.

ST ANDREWS

RICHMOND, STATEN ISLAND

ONE of the most desirable classes of immigrants into the New Netherlands before the establishment of English rule was the Huguenot element that settled along the eastern shore of Staten Island. After the Revocation of the Edict of Nantes in 1685 men and women of this faith came over the seas in increasing numbers, and a chaplain from the fort on Manhattan Island visited them from time to time to hold religious service in French, or for their Dutch neighbours in the language of the Netherlands, the form of worship in either case being that of the Established Church of England.

The little church organised about this time at Richmond was the first on Staten Island. It was called St. Andrew's, and regular services were held in it during the last quarter of the seventeenth century. The first church building was erected in the reign of Queen Anne of England, who sent out the Reverend Eneas McKenzie in 1706 with a silver communion service, which the little parish still numbers among its treasures and memorabilia.

The prosperity of the parish was not long in giving rise to some jealousy among the Dutch residents of Staten Island. Mr. McKenzie accordingly imported from Europe copies of the Book of Common Prayer printed in Dutch, which so pleased the Staten Island Dutch that discord was forever banished. Indeed, in a letter written in 1748 to the Synod of the Dutch Reformed Church in Holland we read that " on Staten Island, within the last twenty years, the Dutch Church has lost half its members. Our people mix with the English, who have an Episcopal Church, and the Dutch Church is in danger of extinction."

In 1711 St. Andrew's parish received a gift of a building site and a burying ground, and two years later a Dutch nabob, by name Adolphus Philipse, with the Mayor of New York, Ebenezer Wilson, jointly contributed one hundred and fifty acres. The proceeds from the sale of this land enabled the parish to acquire a more suitable location for a glebe; and in the same year, 1713, to put up a substantial structure of stone. The earlier church edifice was torn down, as was also in time the newer structure, both of which had occupied the site upon which now stands a later church building, dating from before the American Revolution.

Like some other old churches, St. Andrew's
has been the scene of battles as well as prayer.
The "Queen's Rangers," of the British Army,
were encamped in the village of Richmond in
1776, and the Battle of Richmond was fought
in and about St. Andrew's Church. On August 8, 1777, a detachment of the Continental
Army crossed the Kill von Kull, and marched to
Richmond, where they were met by a party of
British. A slight resistance ensued, after which
the British retreated down the hill to St. Andrew's and took refuge inside its walls. The
Americans after riddling every pane of glass in
the windows with their rapid fire advanced still
closer and continued discharging their volleys
into the church through the windows until every
man of the British was either killed or driven
out of the building.

In course of time St. Andrew's became the
mother of some of the most active of later Protestant Episcopal parishes, not only on Staten
Island, but elsewhere as well. The Reverend
Richard Channing Moore went from St. Andrew's in 1814 to serve the interests of the
Church as Bishop of Virginia. St. Mary's
Chapel of the Church of the Ascension at West
Brighton was an off-shoot, and the beautiful
edifice in which the parish of St. John's Church
worships at Clifton was built to accommodate

parishioners of St. Andrew's residing in that vicinity.

The venerable house of worship of St. Andrew's is still eminent in the religious life of Staten Island, the parish maintaining simple but progressive methods in the " good fight of faith," and constantly recruiting new members. The original charter of the parish, the old prayer books, the pulpit cover, the quaint silver communion service, and the old bell, all of them sent over as tokens of good will by Queen Anne in 1706, are still guarded zealously as memorials of a spiritual and material past that the parishioners regard as not without its glory.

OLD MISSION CHURCH

MACKINAC ISLAND, MICHIGAN

SOME of the most fascinating chapters of American history are those which Francis Parkman made his own, and some of the most interesting passages of those chapters deal with the Island of Mackinaw, or Mackinac. Situated in the Straits of Mackinac, on a highway of the Great Lakes, it has been since the seventeenth century the scene of operations by Indians, Jesuit missionaries, explorers, *coureur des bois* and *voyageurs,* as well as agents of the great Astor Fur Company; while British and American soldiers have successively occupied the white fort on the hillside, built in 1783. Washington Irving in " Astoria " gives a vivid picture of Mackinaw in these early days.

The island continued a centre of population and trade for many years, and its Indians in time attracted the attention of the outside world as a missionary field. In 1820 the Reverend Dr. Jedidiah Morse, a minister of the Congregational faith, and father of the inventor of the telegraph, was commissioned by the United States Government to visit Mackinaw and report

First Presbyterian Church, Newark, New Jersey

San Miguel Church, Santa Fé, New Mexico

the hour of his triumph, De Vargas on the following day gave thanks to the Virgin Mary, to whose assistance he ascribed his victory.

The conquerors soon set about repairing the church of San Miguel. Though wantonly devastated by the Indians, its massive walls were still standing, and by 1710 the restoration of the building was completed. In commemoration of this event an inscription was placed upon one of the vigas near the door of the church, bearing this announcement:

"El Señor Marques de la Penuela hizo esta fabrica. El Alferes Real Don Agustin Flores Vergara su criao ano de 1710." ("The Marquis de la Penuela erected this building. The Royal Ensign Don Agustin Flores Vergara his servant. The year 1710.")

The restorers of San Miguel utilised the original massive walls of adobe, and covered the church with a heavy roof, made of strong vigas, which were supported at each end by carved timbers. An old copper bell, cast in 1350, hangs in the rude belfry.

Inside the church, among many other interesting relics, a number of paintings of religious subjects are still preserved, such as St. Michael and the Dragon, and the Annunciation, some of them containing holes which were pierced in their canvas by arrows during the Indian fights in the old days.

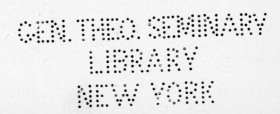